MW00423117

Advanced Praise for
Uncompromising

"Steve White's *Uncompromising* story challenges all of us who may be leaning back with a relaxed approach, to lean forward with ferocity and focus. Only the truly committed will enjoy a fulfilling life and a lasting legacy. I can't think of a leader who wouldn't benefit from pushing the purpose pedal and applying Steve's hard-won life lessons."

—WALT RAKOWICH, *Former CEO, Prologis*

"*Uncompromising* tells the compelling story of Steve White's journey from growing up in poverty to becoming one of America's most successful business leaders and directors. Throughout his career, Steve has combined an extraordinary work ethic with the astute ability to identify the things that truly make the difference to success both in business and, more importantly, in life. With deeply personal stories, Steve identifies essential pathways to a life with true purpose and meaning. These pathways can lead to greater prosperity and shared success for us all. Steve's dedication to helping others live a better and uncompromising life is an inspiration to us all."

—D.G. MACPHERSON, *Chairman & CEO, W.W. Grainger Inc.*

"As a former public company CEO, I was once described as a learning machine by one of my board members who was attributing that strength to my success, so Steve's chapter about 'living life as a learning lab' particularly resonated with me. My personal experience with Steve is that he, too, is a learning machine and he lives this philosophy, always asking many questions, seeking to understand, absorbing and considering new ideas and ways of thinking. Now I understand how he evolved those skills and why he has been successful. A very relatable and meaningful read."

—*LARISSA HERDA, Former Chair and CEO of Time Warner Telecom Inc.*

"Keeping your eye on the prize is the key to every goal we hope to accomplish. Through seven critical life pathways, Steve White shares what it means to have your eye on the real prize and how to avoid losing your way with the short-term distractions of lesser value."

—*SHELLYE ARCHAMBEAU, Fortune 500 Board Director and Author of* Unapologetically Ambitious

"In *Uncompromising*, Steve White delivers the message that 'the path to an impactful life and a lasting legacy is paved by an unwavering commitment to your why,' a concept that I have lived by for most of my life. Through powerful stories of his past, his present, the lives of his mentors and those who have shaped (and continue to shape) him, Steve inspires you to look for the good, be grateful for what you have, and never compromise on who you are. No matter what your personal journey looks like, you will be able to identify with the struggles, successes, celebrations, and life lessons Steve so articulately details, and these stories will become powerful tools for you to apply in your own life, knowing that if you believe it, you truly can achieve it."

—*JIM CRAIG, 1980 Olympic Gold Medalist, President & CEO of Gold Medal Strategies*

"Life is full of uncertain times, twists and turns. Today's business climate is no exception. The uncompromising focus that carried Steve White through troubled waters as a young adult to the terra firma he's worked tirelessly to cultivate as one of America's trusted leaders, is something we should all strive to model as we aim to make our mark and leave a legacy."

—*Brad Shaw, Chairman & CEO, Shaw Communications Inc.*

"Steve White has given us access to his personal life story and his incredible journey to the executive suite. His book is a must-read on so many levels, especially for anyone looking to realize their true potential. Hard hitting at times with raw passion, we see the man who deeply loves his family commit to success and then get it done without compromise. This is an incredible life story. You will ask yourself 'What is my why?' when you finish the book."

—*Robert E. Knowling Jr., Former CEO of Covad Communications Group, and Chairman of Eagles Landing Partners*

"When Steve White talks about life or work, I listen. Whether in the boardroom or over a meal, Steve's uncompromising intellectual curiosity creates profound and provocative conversations, always with the goal of improving focus and results. This book is a terrific compilation of his guiding principles and a fascinating look at the internal compass that guides and drives him."

—*Jim Snee, Chairman, President, and CEO of Hormel Foods Inc.*

"Whether you are a seasoned business executive or a twenty-two-year-old just entering the workforce, *Uncompromising* contains life-changing lessons and reminders. My personal favorites are pathways six and seven. Steve engages the reader by drawing deeply from his own personal struggles and successes. True to the premise of the book, Steve does not make excuses and seeks always to point out the learnings and opportunities. As a board colleague at one of America's most successful food companies, I have watched Steve actually put to work many of the lessons in a real-world setting. The seven pathways are more than just slogans, and Steve walks the talk. These are lessons we can all learn from, and Steve's experiences make him uniquely qualified to share them."

—*GARY BHOJWANI, CEO of CNO Financial Group Inc.*

"Steve gets it! The power of the commitment to your why is your fuel through times of turbulence to continue to steadily march, sometimes run, with ferocity toward your destination. This is a book and daily empowerment to be read over and over again."

—*MICHAEL B. HANCOCK, Forty-Fifth Mayor of Denver, Colorado*

"Page for page, *Uncompromising* is brimming with highs, lows, and everything in between that happens to someone who's on a mission to live a purpose-filled life. If you want one too, you have this book in your hands."

—*CHAUNCEY BILLUPS, Head Basketball Coach, Portland Trail Blazers, and Former NBA Basketball Player*

uncompromising

How an Unwavering Commitment to Your Why
Leads to an Impactful Life and a Lasting Legacy

Steven A. White

Post Hill
PRESS

A POST HILL PRESS BOOK
ISBN: 978-1-63758-239-8
ISBN (eBook): 978-1-63758-240-4

Uncompromising:
How an Unwavering Commitment to Your Why Leads to an Impactful
Life and a Lasting Legacy
© 2022 by Steven A. White
All Rights Reserved

Cover design by Tony Steck

Post Hill Press
New York · Nashville
posthillpress.com

Published in the United States of America
1 2 3 4 5 6 7 8 9 10

To my wife, Barbita,

whose uncompromising approach to what matters has
been and still is a source of motivation and inspiration.

Contents

Acknowledgments

I WAS INSPIRED TO WRITE this book because I've been blessed beyond my wildest expectations. My blessings have not been money, career success, or something else materially, but a life filled with incredible role models and influencers. My journey can best be summed up with the following quote:

> "If you want to go fast, go alone; if you want to go far, go together."

My life has been shaped and influenced by two incredible women. I received an incredible foundation from my mom. Her focus on what matters, her uncompromising approach to life, her risk-taking, her work ethic, her love of God, and her commitment to her why of raising four boys provided a north star for me that still shines today. I also owe a debt of gratitude to my departed stepfather, Smitty, who was a much-needed role model to a small child missing his dad.

My wife, Barbita, has fingerprints on more chapters than she will ever know. I owe every success and accomplishment to her. Barbita's hard truths, her focus on excellence, and her belief in me when I didn't always believe in myself has guided me through every important chapter of my life. She also gave me the greatest gift a man could ever desire—my son, Steven (Stevie) Andrew White II.

Stevie, you have enriched our lives in a way that is difficult to describe. I am so proud of you, and I'm excited for what's to come. You have a very bright future and please know that Dad will always be there for you.

A special shout-out to my three brothers, Linton, Keith, and Anthony (Tony). As the oldest, you allowed me to lead, even when I didn't know how to lead. Your patience and love still inspires me today. My extended family also has been a source of inspiration. From Georgia to Indianapolis to Detroit and back to Florida...I acknowledge your impact on me. Thank you!

I am so blessed to have three lifelong friends in Stanford (Lukie) Miller, Ron Singletary, and Teddy Snowden. While there were times we were not always connected, I never doubted your love and support. You are my "road dogs"!

My pastor Randy Hall played a significant role in assisting me with my moral compass and challenging me to stay true to my reason for being on this earth. May he rest in peace.

To all my friends, I appreciate you because each of you, in some way, shaped me. There are too many names to mention, but "I see you" and acknowledge you.

I also want to recognize my work partners at American Hospital Supply/Convertors, PepsiCo, Colgate Palmolive, and especially my teammates at Comcast. The last twenty years at Comcast have shaped me and provided me the platform to really grow as a leader. A special recognition to Dave Watson, currently CEO of Comcast Cable. Every important career moment for me at Comcast was "touched" by Dave. Your friendship, support, tough love, and steady hand impacted me more than you will ever know. Thank you!

As I outline in the book, I have more mentors than anyone could imagine. The majority didn't even know they were mentoring me as I learned to watch, learn, and grow.

This book is a reality because of my outstanding agent, Michael Palgon. Your tough love and early guidance in crafting my story was just what I needed and I greatly appreciate you. My thanks also go to Denise McMahan, who has been instrumental in helping me evolve my message as I contemplated what I had to share. Stephen Caldwell was extraordinary in assisting me to get the right words on the pages of this book. You are terribly gifted, and I'm glad to call you my writing partner but most importantly my friend. And, finally, to Tommy Spaulding, the *New York Times* bestselling author who gave me the confidence that a book resided inside of me.

I also would like to acknowledge you. Thank you for taking the time to read my story, and I trust my words will inspire, motivate, and help you reach your table of prosperity.

It's been said that the two most important days in your life are the day you were born and the day you find out why. Thank you, God, for blessing me with the insight on why I was placed on this earth: to create a table of prosperity for others by serving them.

Preface

Thriving in My Exhaustion

ONE OF THE GREATEST CHALLENGES of my life can be summed up in a single word: *exhaustion*. I don't know if that's a bad thing, and, in fact, I believe there are times when it can be a good thing. But I know for certain that it's a very real thing and that it played a very real role in why I wrote this book.

I'm not talking about the exhaustion that comes from a hard day of work or even from a stretch when life seems unusually stressful, although I've certainly experienced that, too. In 2020, for instance, the pressures of leading my family and serving as president of the West Division of Comcast Cable were particularly acute. The pandemic, natural disasters, and social unrest all collided during a tumultuous presidential election year. It was a tiring time for most people in the world, me included.

What I'm talking about, however, is more cumulative in nature—not just weeks or months or even years, but a lifetime in the making. It's what some would label as the "burden of my black experience." And the only way I know how to sum it up is with that one word: *exhaustion*.

This isn't a book about race or a book written just for a black audience. It's a book about an uncompromising approach that will help anyone, regardless of race or gender or any other factor, get more meaning out of life. But you will see evidence of my exhaustion woven throughout these pages, so I believe understanding a little about my experience will provide some context that will help make my message more personal, more meaningful, and more relevant to your own journey.

Unlike many people in America, including several I've known, I have never experienced a defining moment that I would link to racism. I haven't been immune to racism, but I have never been roughed up by the police or overtly mistreated by coworkers for no other reason than I was born with black skin. In fact, my most personal experience with overt racism happened one evening about forty years ago when some friends and I stopped in Martinsville, Indiana, to fill up with gas while driving home from college.

Martinsville had a reputation as a racist community, primarily because of the 1968 murder of Carol Jenkins-Davis. She was a young black woman who was selling encyclopedias door-to-door in the small town when someone bludgeoned her with a screwdriver. Kenneth Richmond, a man who was passing through and didn't actually live in Martinsville, was arrested and charged with the crime, but not until thirty-four years after it happened. That's when his daughter came forward and said she had witnessed the slaying as a seven-year-old. But Richmond died before going to trial, so he was never convicted.

We didn't know any of that, of course, when we stopped for gas. All we knew was the town's reputation, and that was enough to make us a little nervous. And, unfortunately, it lived up to our low expectations. When we discovered that the pump wasn't working and mentioned that fact to the attendant at the station, he responded by using the n-word while suggesting that we dig some gas out of the ground. We chose a different option and found another place to fill up the tank.

Other than that episode, I've been fortunate when it comes to avoiding blatant encounters of racism. The realities that come with being black in a mostly white corporate America, however, impacted me in subtle ways that wore on me over time. So, my exhaustion has come from decades of grinding out a path to a better life in light of those realities.

For starters, I have felt exhausted from what often seemed like a never-ending battle to get ahead. Many people, white and black, have shown me grace and poured into my life in ways small and large that helped me see the goodness of humanity, but I've also felt the near-constant winds of resistance from others. There have been days when it felt like people wouldn't give me the benefit of the doubt, that there weren't very many people rooting for me to win, or that some people were actively working to make me lose.

Again, it typically wasn't overt, but there was just enough evidence to make me wonder and tempt me to cast blame or accusation or, worse, give up.

I knew that some of my battle was born from reality—from the systemic inequality of bad policies, bad systems, and, occasionally, bad people. And I knew, intellectually, that part of the battle was created by my perceptions. But it was all real to me, and it made the journey a grind. I felt certain that what took years to build could disappear in an instant. There was never a day when I thought I could let up—when I didn't feel like I had to dress nicer and work longer, harder, and smarter than everyone else around me or else...poof! Gone.

At the same time, my successes in life—as a husband, father, friend, and corporate executive—didn't happen on my own, and I have a tremendous sense of gratitude for those men and women (of all skins colors) who helped me fight through the exhaustion and find my way forward. Ironically, however, that's also another factor in my fatigue—I've always felt a pressure to succeed and give back.

There was (and still is) an unwritten code in the black community when I was growing up that said if you make something good out of your life, you owed a debt to those who paved a path for you—and you better make a payment. It's a philosophy rooted in the idea that to whom much is given much is expected, and it is the heartbeat of progress.

When I look into the black community today, I see success stories in arts, entertainment, sports, academics, science, business, and politics. I also see the absentee fathers, the high incarceration rates for black males, the black-on-black crime, and the systemic racism and failed policies of politicians of every persuasion.

Most of all, however, I see hope and opportunity.

We've come a long way, but we can do better. We *must* do better. Society has its part to play. Politicians have their part to play. But it starts by looking in the mirror. We've all been given what we need to make a positive difference in a world—to build a life that matters for ourselves and to others. And for as long as I can remember, I've felt a deep sense of responsibility to do my part.

When it became clear I had a chance to get out of the inner city and all of its negative trappings, I felt the weight of my race on my shoulders. Some call this black guilt. *Don't let your race down.* Whatever you call it, I felt I had to succeed for myself and my family, but also for all African Americans past, present, and future.

Not only that, but I felt the pressure to avoid failures or even show signs of weakness that would give ammunition to the critics.

The message I heard loud and clear, even if it wasn't always spoken, went something like this: *People died for you to have the opportunities you are getting. They died so you can go in any restaurant you want to eat in. They died so you can vote. They died so you can go to college. They died so you can get a job in the corporate world. They died so you can buy a house in a nice neighborhood. They died, in short, so you can have it better than they had it. If you don't make good on your opportunities, you are letting down all those folks who sacrificed for you. And if you do make good, you better pay it forward.*

Many trailblazers, of course, didn't die for me, but they all sacrificed in ways that benefited me. I never knew most of them. They stood up for me by marching arm-in-arm across bridges, sitting in seats in the forbidden front of a bus, writing letters from a jail cell, preaching from a podium on the public square, and debating for policy changes everywhere from the city halls in Middle America to the halls of Congress in Washington, DC.

Others came alongside me during my journey, from the white people who tipped me when I was an eleven-year-old with a paper route based on the quality of my service rather than the color of my skin to the teachers, coaches, mentors, friends, and family members who lovingly helped me along my way.

I wrote this book partly to pay my debt to those people—not to pay it off, because that's not possible, but to make a payment toward it. I have a responsibility, but I also feel genuinely grateful. I see this book as sort of my love letter to the people who have given me a hand up. What better way to recognize them and honor them than by sharing with the world what they taught me? What better way to pay it forward?

That's what makes my exhaustion fade into the background—the fact that the day-in, day-out grind could wear me down, but it could never wear me out.

I've come to recognize the reality that all of us are dealing with something—our own unique obstacles and trials that shape us. But while my exhaustion shaped me, it doesn't define me. It's my response to it that defines me, and I'm eager to share what I've learned, both from my successes and my mistakes, about the pathways that have helped me overcome it.

My hope is that no matter your race, no matter your background, and no matter what challenges are shaping your experience, this book will open your heart and mind to an uncompromising approach to a better life. It won't eliminate your grind, but I truly believe it will help you find contentment and purpose in your journey.

Chapter 1

My Uncompromising Start—
Why I Believe What I Believe

THERE CAME A POINT WHEN I was around ten years old that I realized I wasn't spending my weekends like most other kids.

As far as I could tell, other kids all slept as late as they wanted on Saturdays and then watched *Scooby-Doo* until someone fixed them a big bowl of Cheerios. After breakfast, they got dressed and took off to play with friends in that wonderland known as the imagination. For the rest of the day, they were explorers in Africa, pirates on the high seas, soldiers building forts, or sports stars hitting game-winning shots.

Me? I was in a motel room.

As much as any other experience from my formative years, those weekends at the motel would shape what I came to believe, how I would approach life, and the husband, father, and leader that I would become. At the time, however, they were a pain in the...

Well, let's just say I didn't always see the value in it.

Lanie Mae White saw the value, not to mention the necessity.

For three full years beginning in the summer of 1971, she would wake up early on those weekends, rouse my brothers and me from our slumber, and get us fed and dressed. Then she would pack us into the car for a ten-mile drive from our small home in Indianapolis to the Quality Inn across from the Indiana State Fairgrounds.

The fairgrounds were a magical place for many visitors. The state fair took place in August, but people came to the northwest corner of 38th Street and Fall Creek Parkway all year round for a variety of events. The Indiana Farmers Coliseum, as it's now known, was the centerpiece. It opened in 1939, and it has hosted concerts featuring everyone from Tennessee Ernie Ford to the Beatles. In 1971, there were performances by Neil Diamond, the Jackson 5, Santana, Red Skelton, and Frank Zappa. At the time, the venue also was home to the NBA's Indiana Pacers, not to mention boat shows, boxing matches, an assortment of festivals, and multiple commencement ceremonies.

From my perspective, all those events had one thing in common: they were attended by people who made a helluva mess at the Quality Inn—and my mom had to clean it up.

Momma was a maid, and my brothers and I spent most of our weekends as her little helpers.

The Quality Inn was a motel with an "m," not hotel with an "h." You know the difference, right? There are no interior hallways at a motel. You can see the doors to the rooms from the parking lot under the neon sign that glows with the rates for the night. And there is no elevator, no fitness room, and no spa.

This particular motel was as bare-bones as bare-bones could get. The guests tended to treat it like it was a fraternity house and they were partying with John Belushi. They left a wake a mile wide and two miles deep—beer cans, broken liquor bottles, drug paraphernalia, dirty clothes, leftover food, and anything else they didn't want or happened to forget.

Momma never complained, and she never let us complain, either. She made the beds, scrubbed the bathrooms, and picked up the nastiest trash you can imagine—and some that defied imagination.

When she first took the job, my brothers and I would sit quietly for hours where the maids washed the linens and kept their supplies. We weren't allowed to play in the parking lot or watch television in the rooms. We had no "screens" to watch or for playing games.

As the oldest, I was in charge, but we all really knew that Momma was in charge—even when she wasn't right there.

"Sit down and behave," we were told, "or Momma will get fired."

So we sat and, surprisingly, we were well behaved— at least well enough that she didn't get fired. Eventually, however, we tagged along and helped Momma with her duties. We brought her supplies from her cart, picked up trash, took care of our baby brother when he came on the scene, and did other menial tasks to keep us occupied.

Along the way, we also soaked in the examples our mother modeled with her hard work and quiet pride in a job well done. I pouted and complained about being there, especially about changing my brother's cloth diapers, but I also came to appreciate Momma's courage and the fullness of her sacrifices.

In many ways, it was right there in that motel that I began learning the lessons that would shape my beliefs for the rest of my life. But to understand those lessons, you also need to know how and why my mother got to that motel in the first place.

A LIFE-ALTERING DECISION

Momma was a thirty-year-old divorced African American woman with an eighth-grade education and very little work experience when she left most of her family and friends in southern Georgia and moved to Indianapolis for a fresh start.

She had grown up in Upson County, Georgia, about two hours south of Atlanta. It's not the end of the world, but, as the saying goes, you could see it from there. In 1954, at fourteen, she walked the aisle of the Salem Baptist Church to take the preacher by the hand and give her life to Jesus. Five years later, at nineteen, she walked that aisle again, this time to marry my father, Linton White Sr.

Jesus never left her side; my dad, not so much.

At first, things were just fine. They moved to Orange Park, Florida, to start their family, and that's where I was born in December 1960. Two more sons soon followed, Linton Jr. and Keith.

Daddy was an auto mechanic for B.F. Goodrich. He'd get up early and come home tired and dirty from a full, hard day on the job. Momma worked briefly—just for a few weeks, as she recalls—cleaning the homes of middle-class white families. She didn't care for it, she once told me, but she especially didn't like how the to-do list would grow once she arrived while the pay always stayed the same.

She soon returned to her role as homemaker, but those few weeks when she worked stand out for me because that was when I realized we weren't wealthy. I remember walking to school and passing a nice but modest house where a kid named Scott lived. He had blond hair and sat in the front row of my first-grade class, and I mainly remember him for two reasons. One, the teacher almost always called on him when she asked questions, and, two, Momma had cleaned his house. The teacher seldom called on me, and we definitely didn't have anyone coming over to clean our house.

Even though I knew we weren't wealthy, I never felt we lacked the things we needed. I didn't go to bed hungry. I never felt mistreated or unloved. And as far as I could tell, our parents were happily married.

Later, I learned that Daddy started hanging out with coworkers who drank, something he didn't do at all when my parents first married. Before long, as Momma puts it, "He got on the wrong road and lost his way." He sank deeper into the bottle and soon lost his job. My mother, whose father had been an alcoholic, eventually made up her mind that she wouldn't raise her sons in that type of home. It was the toughest decision of her life, and it would radically alter mine.

Momma and Daddy protected us from whatever dys-function scarred their relationship—we never heard argu-ments or saw any bottles thrown across the room—so it took me by surprise when they divorced.

I had just turned ten. Like many boys that age, I idol-ized my dad. I remember him as a strong, silent type—a stoic, six-foot-three-inch-tall man who could fix anything and never let on that he had a care in the world. I was dev-astated to leave him and my friends with three months left in my fifth-grade year. He came to visit us a few times in Georgia, perhaps trying to woo my mom back to Florida, and he no doubt would have gotten my vote for that if any-one had asked.

Then things went from bad to worse, at least from my perspective. After finishing the 1971 spring semester in Upson County, Momma announced that we were moving to Indianapolis. It was then that I began to understand just how fiercely independent my mother really was.

Most of her family and my father's family lived in rural Georgia, but she had a brother, my Uncle Horace, who lived in Indianapolis. Momma knew her relatives and for-mer in-laws in Georgia would share in the raising of her boys if she stayed, and she feared that we would end up split apart—one living here, another there. She had left Florida with a plan, I later learned, and that plan was to move to Indiana and raise her sons with limited interfer-ence from others.

She was told by friends and family that such a move was a terrible mistake. She knew nothing about raising boys, they said. She had no job, they pointed out. The temptations of the big city would pull her boys away from her, they predicted. They won't amount to anything if you move them, she heard. They will fall into trouble, they said, and end up in jail—or worse.

Her response? She left all her furniture in Georgia with my uncles Pete and O.B., and they drove her and her three boys to the bus station. Then, with nothing but the clothes that would fit in a few suitcases and $500 she had squirreled away, we boarded a Greyhound northbound for Indiana.

Other than a few phone calls, I had little interaction with my father after we moved. He died in December 1977 when he was thirty-seven and I was just a few weeks shy of my seventeenth birthday. My life wasn't greatly influenced by his presence, but my exhaustion definitely was shaped by his absence.

A MODEL OF SACRIFICE

When we arrived in Indiana, we lived with Uncle Horace and his family for three weeks until we moved into a duplex that we called a "double-home"—there were two front doors and a thin wall separating the two apartments that were both so small you could roll a bowling ball through the front door and out the back without hitting a thing.

A couple of years later, we "upgraded" to an apartment in the housing projects. And a few years after that, Momma had saved enough to buy a 1,200-square-foot three-bedroom home with one bathroom and a one-car garage that we later converted into a family room. Momma lived at that home on Meadowlark Drive until late in 2020. By then, the neighborhood had changed dramatically, and, for her safety, we finally convinced her to move.

Life was never what you'd consider easy for my mother when we were growing up, but it was particularly challenging during those first few years in Indy. She was determined to make it on her own, so when one of Uncle Horace's friends mentioned that the Quality Inn was hiring, she filled out an application and landed the first steady job she'd ever had.

Uncle Horace found her a deal on a used but amazingly reliable car, and she parted ways with her $500 nest egg so she would have transportation.

Not long after she started working, Momma learned she was pregnant with my youngest brother, Anthony, who would arrive on my birthday in December 1972.

With one more mouth to feed, she scrimped and saved, stretching every dollar as far as it could go and then some. We lived within her income and never, as she put it, had "big eyes" for things we couldn't afford. That meant we got the essentials, but Christmas and birthdays didn't always include gifts. In fact, she tells the story of one Christmas when all we got was some apples, peaches, and oranges that she paid for with ten dollars I donated from my earnings delivering newspapers.

My brothers and I learned to work, and not just at the motel. We had picked peaches during the summers back in Georgia, earning a robust twenty-five cents per basket, and I took the paper route almost as soon as we arrived in Indiana. Uncle Horace also had a side business hauling away people's junk on the weekends, and sometimes he'd pay us five dollars to ride along and help.

Because her paycheck was small and my uncle and his family were the only relatives within six hundred miles of us, Momma didn't have many options when it came to childcare. Once we were in school, we went to the nearby boys and girls club on weekday afternoons. We had a key to our home, and we usually let ourselves in before Momma got back to fix us dinner. But on the weekends and during the summer, we typically were her sidekicks at the motel until 1974, which was when she got a job as a janitor at a high school and I got a job at a Burger Chef.

In addition to working on the weekends, we also spent a good amount of time at the Traveler's Rest Baptist Church, where the Reverend Charles Bledsoe presided over about a hundred congregants and where my Aunt Alfa played the organ. We were there on Sundays and Wednesdays, as well as for assorted other special occasions.

I joined the church and was baptized when I was thirteen, but it was years later before my faith became central to my life. For my mother, faith was always essential. In the days and nights after her divorce, she prayed one simple prayer—*Lord, just let me live to see my children grow up*—while rememorizing and reciting verses from Psalms 23, 27, and 37 for comfort and reassurance as she cried herself to sleep.

She wasn't praying for us to go to college or to become wealthy, she later told me; she just wanted us to survive until adulthood, become responsible, hardworking men, and find jobs that would allow us to provide for our families. Her goal wasn't that we'd become rich and famous but that we'd stay alive and maybe, just maybe, break the cycles of generational poverty and family dysfunction.

The odds certainly were stacked against my mother, and there were many times when she failed or was knocked down by life. But there never was a doubt that her faith made her stronger than her circumstances, that she wouldn't be defined by her mistakes, and that her four sons would swim in lakes of opportunity rather than wallow in cesspools of racial or class stereotypes.

She taught us about hard work and self-reliance, what it meant to take risks for something you truly believed in, how to steer clear of the things that might cause us harm, and why faith in God was the key to joy and contentment. She set rules and gave us firm boundaries, many of which we fought hard against, only to realize later that they saved us from the pain of our ignorance. When we did well, she praised us. And when we didn't toe the line, she administered some old-school discipline.

As a result, my brothers and I had no excuse not to achieve whatever version of success we decided to pursue. It was up to us to make the most of those opportunities, and, for the most part, we did. We all faced obstacles, some from within and some that weren't of our making, but we all rose to the challenges, persevered, and overcame.

For me, the twists and turns in a journey that began with a broken home in the Deep South and veered north to the projects of Indianapolis somehow resulted in a college degree, an amazing marriage, a miracle son, and positions of leadership in corporate America. Eventually, as president of Comcast West, I was responsible for thirty thousand employees across thirteen states and a business that generated more than $18 billion in annual revenue.

Success for my brothers has looked different, of course, but it's been no less meaningful, especially in the eyes of our mother. Linton is a chief financial officer who has been married twenty-eight years to Jennifer and has two kids. Keith is a confirmed bachelor who retired after a career as a high school custodian. And Anthony, the youngest, works for Comcast, has been married for eleven years to Tammy, and has one child.

In 1994, when Momma was diagnosed with colon cancer, she told the surgeon she "couldn't complain" if she didn't survive because by that time, God had answered her prayer. Her boys were grown and doing just fine. They did the surgery anyway, of course, and she emerged without a trace of the cancer remaining. "If you die," the surgeon told her, "it won't be from this cancer."

FINE-TUNING MY BELIEFS

While I owe much of my success in life to the lessons and values I learned while cleaning motel rooms with Momma, obviously it didn't all happen there. The things I believe have been shaped by a combination of experiences from my upbringing, my marriage, and my career. I believe what I believe, in other words, because of what I learned from being poor for twenty-five years, from being married for thirty-plus years, and from leading others for more than thirty-five years.

That feels like three lifetimes of experiences!

Some insights came early, while others took much more time and often involved the school of hard knocks—not just the circumstances that were beyond my control but the consequences of my poor decisions and mistakes that at times resulted in sizable failures in both my personal and professional life. All of those experiences, the good and the bad, ignited my passion to be my best and eventually fueled my desire to help others be their best.

No one has played a bigger role in my story, of course, than my wife.

Barbita Webster entered the picture when I was twenty-nine, just in time to become the rudder I had no idea I needed. I was a regional manager for Pepsi with a nice townhouse in Norfolk, Virginia, and no real interest in a long-term relationship. She was a young, on-the-rise executive with IBM.

Barbita called one afternoon at the prompting of one of our mutual friends. It was 4:38 p.m. eastern standard time on May 11, 1990, and I already had plans for the night. But there was something in her voice during that five-minute call that drew me in like the song of the siren, and I convinced her to meet me for a late dinner at a restaurant in the Hilton Hotel. Then I told my other date something had come up and I could only meet her for drinks.

I showed up early for dinner and watched several women come in as I sat in the lobby. Then, at 8:11 p.m., to be precise, a stunningly beautiful lady walked toward me. A thought shot through my head: *Whatever she's asking, the answer is yes.* Thankfully, she said, "Are you Steve?"

Needless to say, she made a great first impression. And a lasting one as well. I bungled things a few times at the start, but she offered grace and soon we became inseparable.

On October 7 of that same year, we eloped and were married on a beach in Maui. Since our family wasn't there, we sprung for an all-out video package, and a crew was filming us as we walked from the resort to the beach, me in my black tux and her looking stunning in her white wedding dress.

We quickly captured the attention of the other vacationers. A television soap opera had been filming at the hotel earlier that week, and the guests assumed this was just another scene. Around three hundred of them, in fact, followed us to the beach and witnessed our nuptials!

It's impossible to overstate how significant Barbita has been in helping me win at life the right way. First, she has sacrificed many times for my success, passing up opportunities to advance her corporate career to support me in my journey—which became our journey. And when I felt the weight of expectations, she encouraged me with invaluable insights and perspective.

Second, she held me accountable to our values. When I briefly experimented with drugs when we were dating, she told me, in no uncertain terms, that she would not go on that ride with me. When my faith in God wavered and my priorities became too self-focused, she not only prayed for me but nudged me, often gently and sometimes with more force, until I found my way back to the true path.

Other values were modeled for me along the way by teachers, friends, and mentors in my personal and professional life who would pour into me, chiseling away the bad and helping reshape the good into something better. You'll meet many of these people and the values they lived and taught in subsequent chapters.

Of course, none of them owned my decisions. They prepared the table and gave me a seat, but it was up to me to eat. And, thankfully, I typically thought what they were serving looked really good, so I tucked in my napkin, picked up my fork, and chowed down. Now I'm inviting you to that same table.

YOUR UNCOMPROMISING WHY

Odds are that you aren't a single mother living in poverty, but I can almost guarantee there are things that stand between you and a life well lived—things that make your experiences more exhausting.

Maybe it's racism (in you or around you). Maybe it's low expectations by your teachers or parents. Maybe it's the pressure to live up to the successes of your parents or siblings. Maybe it's an abusive relationship. Maybe it's an incompetent boss or a backstabbing coworker. Maybe it's just your coziness with the status quo or your fear of getting out of your comfort zone.

Whatever it is, and it probably is more than one obstacle, it will shape your experiences and, therefore, shape what you believe and how you behave.

Regardless of what's standing in your way, I'm convinced you can move past it—over it, under it, around it, or right through it. My mother did it. I did it. And I've known many others who have done it. It's not easy. But you can do it, too—if you adopt an uncompromising approach to your life's why.

That's the heart of my message: the path to an impactful life and a lasting legacy is paved by an unwavering commitment to your why.

What do I mean by *your why*?

It's been said that the two most important days in your life are the day you were born and the day you find out why. Many people go to their graves without ever discerning their reason for existing, and that's not only a shame for them but for all the people they encountered throughout their lives who missed out on the best they had to offer.

My mother figured out why she was placed on this earth—the very thing she was born to achieve—and that's what motivated her to leave my father and move to Indiana. Come hell or high water, she was dead set on building a solid foundation for her sons to escape the relentless cycle of generational poverty and broken families that ensnares all too many would-be victims, especially among African Americans.

That was her why—or her "fight," as I like to call it—and she pursued it with an unwavering commitment. She was fiercely independent. She was radically responsible. She was scrappy. And she would not be distracted.

She was *uncompromising*.

And so, that's how I define uncompromising—a fiercely independent, radically responsible, scrappy, and undistracted mindset with an unwavering commitment to your why.

That is the essence of what I saw in the woman who took us to work with her at a motel, and that aptly describes the path upon which she put me and my brothers.

I realize the notion of an *uncompromising* mindset might seem a bit rigid or intolerant. The art of compromise, after all, has become ingrained as a modern virtue, something worth pursuing in politics, business, marriages, and anything else that involves relationships.

Too often, however, we forget that true success hinges on knowing those areas in life in which we actually *should be* uncompromising—and then *being* uncompromising in those areas. The commitment I'm talking about is to core values that never change. For me, that's my family, my faith, being comfortable in my black skin, and being fully committed to my commitments.

But I recognize that life is a journey with many detours and unforeseeable roadblocks along the way. We make mistakes. We get punched in the gut. We reach milestones that represent success, leading us to think we've "made it." And we also fail even after giving it our all. There are circumstances we can't control, and the goals we pursue are often works in progress. Even our why evolves through the stages of life. So while we need to be uncompromising in our commitment, we have to stay flexible in our methods.

The type of uncompromising approach I'm recommending also isn't intolerant. It's not about asking others to live up to the expectations that we've set for ourselves. At our best, we help others discover their why and pursue it in an uncompromising fashion, but we do that while recognizing the beauty of human diversity and the reality of free will. There's accountability but not judgment.

An uncompromising mindset is forged from our failures and imperfections, so there's no room for boasting. But it's essential to our success, because it motivates us to get up when we've been knocked down, to reorient our direction when we've veered off course, and to walk in gratitude for the blessings of our lives. It is a demanding but aspirational approach—a personal commitment we make knowing that perfection is unattainable but that progress toward a meaningful life and legacy only comes with this daily recommitment to doing our best.

The journey of a life well lived has many stages and takes us many places, and the richness of it comes from learning from both the successes and failures along the way. Frankly, I could not have written this book when I was twenty-three—or thirty-three or forty-three. Even now, I concede that I'm writing what I know based on what I've learned so far and that tomorrow I will learn something new.

Looking back on fifty-plus years of experience, however, I see some significant patterns that form what I believe are seven essential, intertwined pathways to an uncompromising life: finding your fight, focusing on the (real) prize, living life as a learning lab, thinking and acting like a business, owning your attitude and effort, navigating uncertainty, and committing to what I call road-dog relationships.

No matter who we are, where we go, what we do, or how often we get knocked down, we position ourselves for success if we take an uncompromising approach to staying on those pathways.

The best part is that you can reap the rewards that come with such a commitment. They are available to anyone who chooses to adopt a fiercely independent, radically responsible, scrappy, and undistracted mindset with an unwavering commitment to their why—the pastor of a church, the CEO of a public company, the founder of a technology start-up, the professor at a university, the nurse in an emergency room, the stay-at-home mom homeschooling three kids, the executive director of a nonprofit, and, of course, the single mother cleaning motel rooms.

The best practices that help you stay on these pathways lead to an impactful life of positive influence and draw others toward you to collaborate and achieve shared success. They result in deeper fulfillment in your daily journey and a positive impact on your family and your organization.

I'd love for you to join me on this journey, but first you need to take an important step: you must expect success. I am convinced that we are all products of our expectations. Too often, however, we limit our future because we don't really believe in who we are and who we're meant to be. Then we become prisoners of our challenges, whether they are big, defining moments or smaller events that wear us down over time. So an uncompromising life begins with embracing the type of expectations that set us free from our exhaustions.

Chapter 2

Great Expectations—
You Have to Believe to Achieve

ROBERT ROSENTHAL AND LENORE JACOBSON conducted a famous study in the late 1960s that led to what's known as the Pygmalion effect.

If you are into classic Latin literature, you might remember Pygmalion from Book X of Ovid's *Metamorphoses*. Pygmalion was a sculptor who fell in love with the statue of a beautiful woman he carved from ivory. When he quietly wished for a wife in the likeness of the statue, the goddess Aphrodite responded by bringing the statue to life. His expectation became his reality.

Instead of using mythical gods and ivory statues for their research, Rosenthal and Jacobson used something with far more energy—elementary school students. Jacobson was the principal of a school in California, so she and Rosenthal put together a project designed to see how expectations of teachers in her school affected the performance of students.

They tested the students at the beginning of the school year and then told the teachers the names of the 20 percent who showed "unusual potential for intellectual growth."[1] The teachers thought the names were based on the test results, but they actually were chosen at random. At the end of the school year, the students were retested and the random group showed greater increases than the others who hadn't been singled out.

"The change in the teachers' expectations regarding the intellectual performance of these allegedly 'special' children had led to an actual change in the intellectual performance of these randomly selected children," the authors wrote in *Pygmalion in the Classroom*, which has been updated a couple of times since it was first published in 1968.

The lesson: The expectations others have of us affects how they treat us, which affects the expectations we form for ourselves. And the expectations we have of ourselves affect our beliefs and our actions, which, of course, affects our results.

This is a deeply personal topic for me because I know what it's like to feel the discouragement of low expectations—and to feel the burden of high expectations. I've also discovered over time how expectations can free me to overcome my exhaustion and pursue my why.

In fact, I've come to believe that a "fiercely independent, radically responsible, scrappy, and undistracted mindset" around expectations is foundational for anyone who wants to experience meaningful success. And if you don't believe me, just ask Wes Moore—or the other Wes Moore.

1   Robert Rosenthal and Lenore Jacobson, *Pygmalion in the Classroom: Teacher Expectation and Pupils' Intellectual Development* (Norwalk, CT: Crown House Publishing, 2003).

THE OTHER WES MOORE

Wes Moore and I met in January 2020 when he spoke at the WD 500, an annual leadership conference for around five hundred directors and above in the West Division of Comcast Cable. Wes was one of our keynote speakers, and we talked prior to the event so I could get to know him a little better and so we could discuss how his message fit with our theme of "Our Way Forward." I introduced him when it was his turn to take the stage, and then I joined him for a short Q&A session when he finished.

Wes is younger than me, but we share similar backgrounds, and we are both passionate about things like the value of hard work, focus, education, and pursuing your purpose in life. He offered our team several great insights, but the thing that stood out the most to me was his vivid description of the power of expectations—those we set for ourselves, those we set for others, and those that others set for us.

His understanding of expectations was developed from a personal experience that began several years earlier when he learned the story of—get this—another Wes Moore.

The name *Wes Moore* is fairly common (like Steve White, right?), but the intertwined paths of these two Wes Moores ended up making a fascinating case study.

Here's the context:

The Wes Moore who spoke at our conference is a really smart, genuinely likeable guy who is making a positive difference in the world. By almost any measure, he qualifies as a success story. That's why we invited him to speak.

Wes attended prep school at Valley Forge Military Academy and then earned a degree from Johns Hopkins University and was a Rhodes Scholar at Oxford University.

He was a captain and paratrooper with the US Army, seeing combat duty in Afghanistan.

In addition to serving as a White House Fellow to Condoleezza Rice when she was secretary of state, he has found success as an entrepreneur in both the for-profit and nonprofit sectors. He worked in investment banking, founded a tech platform that helps underserved college students, and launched an anti-poverty nonprofit based in New York City. He's also written several books, and, oh by the way, he has TV-star good looks, a wonderful wife, and two kids.[2]

His story takes on a greater meaning when you consider a few facts that don't typically show up on someone's résumé: He was born in one of the toughest neighborhoods of inner-city Baltimore. He was four years old when he watched as his father died from a rare virus. And he was raised by grandparents (in the Bronx) and a single mother (in Baltimore). When he was thirteen, he rebelled and began falling in with the wrong crowd, so his family sent him to a boarding school. It took some time, but Wes eventually redirected his wayward life.

Then there's the *other* Wes Moore. He also was born in Baltimore's inner city, and he, too, had no father in his life (although for different reasons). While they didn't know each other growing up, the two Wes Moore's actually were born within a year of the same date in the early 1970s. And like the Wes Moore who spoke to my team, this Wes Moore also was in and out of trouble with the police during his formative years.

The other Wes Moore, however, didn't turn his life around.

---

2   The biographical information comes from *https://www.robinhood.org/wes-moore/index.html.*

This Wes Moore fathered the first of several children while still a teenager, never graduated from high school, and became entangled in a life of crime. He was twenty-five on February 7, 2000, when he and three other men put on masks, went in a jewelry store, ordered everyone to the floor, and stole $438,000 worth of merchandise.

Their plan hit a snag, however, when Bruce Prothero, a thirty-five-year-old off-duty police officer who was working a second job as a security guard, pursued them into the parking lot. Prothero, who was married and had five children, was shot three times during the ordeal and died from the wounds.[3] The assailants eventually were all arrested and convicted of felony murder. Moore now is serving a life sentence in Maryland's Jessup Correctional Institution.[4]

As it turned out, *The Baltimore Sun* was publishing stories about the jewelry heist and murdered police officer about the same time that it was publishing stories about a local young man who was heading to England as a Rhodes Scholar. And when Wes Moore the Rhodes Scholar read the story of Wes Moore the suspected felon, he went on a journey of self-discovery. It resulted in an ongoing friendship with Wes Moore the inmate and a best-selling book that's appropriately titled, *The Other Wes Moore*.

When I joined Wes on the stage at the famed Broadmoor resort in Colorado Springs, the discussion turned to what had caused such dramatically different outcomes in two lives that began in such amazingly similar fashions. Interestingly, Wes recalled a profound conversation he had

---

3   Wes Moore, *The Other Wes Moore: One Name, Two Fates* (New York: Spiegel & Brau, 2010).
4   Jessica Anderson, "No new trial for man convicted in killing of Balto. Co. officer," *The Baltimore Sun*, June 18, 2013, *https://www.baltimoresun.com/news/crime/bs-md-co-wesley-moore-hearing-20130618-story.html*, last accessed May 20, 2020.

with the other Wes Moore, during which he asked him if he thought they were products of their environments.

"Wes looked at me," Moore told the audience at the conference, "and he said, 'Actually, I think we're products of our expectations.'"

It was an epiphany for Wes and for me, because it drove home the reality that both men had lived up to the expectations that were placed in front of them and that they had embraced for themselves.

"The chilling truth is that his story could have been mine," Wes wrote in the introduction to his book. "The tragedy is that my story could have been his."[5]

Wes believes the "expectation gap" in society is just as dangerous as the education gap or the technology gap, and that to close it we need to ask and answer two fundamental questions: "How do we help people think differently about their lives, and how do we think differently about the lives of others?"[6]

I couldn't agree more. In fact, I believe that how we understand and deal with the expectations of our lives sets us up for whatever journey we end up taking.

We could argue all day and into a million weeks about nature versus nurture. But no matter how those two forces combine to shape us, I am convinced that expectations play a massive role in what becomes of us in life. Whatever road we truly *believe* we can travel on is the road we will inevitably take. That's why it's so important to take uncompromising control of our expectations, not only the ones we have for ourselves but also the ones we have for the people we influence.

---

5   Wes Moore, *The Other Wes Moore: One Name, Two Fates* (New York: Spiegel & Brau, 2010).

6   Also from the video that is available at *www.amazon.com/Other-Wes-Moore-Name-Fates/dp/0385528205*, last accessed May 20, 2020.

MODELS OF EXPECTATIONS

The first people who set expectations for us are our parents, and that certainly was the case for me. I loved my mother from the get-go and always wanted to make her happy, but, like most boys, there was something different about my relationship with my father. I not only wanted to please him, but I wanted to be like him. And so, the expectations he established were particularly meaningful.

In areas like hard work, my father modeled extremely high expectations that remain with me today. Unfortunately, he also sometimes set the bar pretty low. While I felt his love for me, he didn't always set a good example of what it looked like to be an involved, emotionally connected husband and father. I don't recall ever having heartfelt talks that would shape a positive vision for my future. In fact, he didn't talk much at all when he was home. You know how some people love to quote their parents? *My dad always said this....* Or *my mom always said that....* Well, when I complete that sentence it's, *My dad always said...nothing.*

Dad worked hard at his job, but not at our relationship. We didn't do father-son outings. No fishing or camping trips. No catch or basketball in the backyard. And no long chats about girls, school, my friends, my hopes and dreams, or anything else. He was gentle and kind toward me, but he set expectations for me with his actions rather than his words. And I looked up to him because he seemed larger than life.

I often wonder how his life and mine might have been different if we had stayed in Florida or even close by in Georgia. Would my presence in some way have caused him to live differently? Could he have become the type of father I wanted and needed? Or would he have continued on the path he chose to take—and would I have followed in the large footsteps he was making?

I don't remember Dad ever coming to Indianapolis, but I do recall flying to Florida for his funeral. It was 1977, less than ten years after we moved away. Momma flew with me, and my brothers drove with one of our uncles on Dad's side of the family who passed through and picked them up.

I never knew exactly how he died. Did the drinking kill him, or was it from some other circumstances? Was it from a broken heart? Momma and I didn't talk about it, that's for sure. All I really remember about the funeral is that I wore a green three-piece suit and brown shoes as I sat through the service not really knowing how to feel. The connection had been broken years before. There was no relationship. No sense of loss. No tears. Just sadness.

I have forgiven my dad, because I realized he battled issues I'll never really understand, and it's not my place to judge his life. But I also know that his life could have been mine. His examples set expectations that I easily could have adopted for myself.

Even after we moved, it would have been easy for me to have followed his path. After all, there was no shortage of men in Indianapolis who had followed a similar path. The projects were full of broken homes with absentee fathers. Some boys gravitated to gangs, in search of a sense of place. For many of them, crime was the family business. School was nothing more than a way to pass the time until they worked the streets and searched for the next artificial high. Their homes were filled with drinking, drugs, and X-rated behaviors. To a young boy, the no-rules world had a certain allure. And if it was good enough for Dad, well, why not me?

In short, I could have ended up much like the "other" Wes Moore.

Fortunately, there were other people in my life who added to the foundations established by my mother and fed me with expectations that put me on a different pathway. My mother's brothers—and, in particular, my Uncle Horace—modeled many positive qualities for me. And I also owe my higher expectations for myself to teachers like Alice Goodrum and mentors like Coach Ernie Cline.

Alice Goodrum taught speech at Arsenal Technical High School, where around 5,500 kids regularly tested the patience of every educator on the historic inner-city campus. I suspect she found it a little odd at first that a fifteen-year-old son of a janitor parked his rear end in a front-row seat every day, locked eyes with her as she taught, and listened to what she had to say. But I figured it was the best way to learn something from the class, earn a good grade, and make my mother proud.

Ms. Goodrum, it turned out, gave me much, much more than a good grade. She was part of a racially diverse cross-section of people who showed me the goodness of humanity regardless of the color of their skin. While I had many positive black influences among teachers, family, and friends, Ms. Goodrum was one of several white people who helped me see my future.

She was in her sixties by the time I came along, but Ms. Goodrum still had plenty of energy for her students. And she not only poured into us when we were in her classroom, but she occasionally would invite us to her home for some sort of off-campus activity.

The first time I went to her house, I was amazed. It was big, at least compared to what I knew, and it seemed magnificent. What stood out the most to me back then, and it seems sort of strange to me now, was her lawn. I'll never forget her lawn because, well, it actually had grass! Not dirt. Not concrete. Grass.

I thought to myself, *This is how people live?*

That was a defining moment for me because I realized there was a whole other world out there to explore beyond the housing projects. My mother had instilled important values in my life, but much of her focus was on behavior— she insisted that I work hard and stay out of trouble. And I'd received encouragement from others along the way. But now, somehow, my perspective was beginning to shift to a future that was much bigger, broader, and better than anything I'd previously imagined.

When I was back in Florida, for instance, I never thought I could live in a home that was cleaned by a maid. That was for other people. People like Scott. Rich people. My aspirations were modest. I thought the greatest job a person could have was to be a postal carrier. These were men (and they were mostly men in my neighborhood back then) who wore nice uniforms, had positions of responsibility because they were trusted to deliver vital documents, and were respected by the people I knew. Not only that, but the work didn't seem as backbreaking as, say working in a factory, and they earned what in my mind was good money. So for a long time, I believed a job as a postal carrier would be about as good as I could ever expect to get.

As I grew older, I still respected the people who delivered mail, but I realized there were many other career options, and those options weren't limited to a few square miles of Indianapolis. My career dreams morphed several times through the years—NBA superstar, sportscaster, businessperson who makes lots of money, successful leader who creates a table of prosperity for others—but it was people like Ms. Goodrum who helped me see those dreams and, more importantly, to see them as realistic expectations.

It wasn't just that Ms. Goodrum took me to her home; it was also the way she treated me as a student. I never felt like some invisible cog in the educational wheel that she was trying to pass through to the next grade on her way to retirement. She took the time to know me. She called on me to answer questions. She encouraged me when I did well. She told me she knew I was capable of something better when I didn't give my best. And because she was a really good teacher, I gained the self-confidence that comes from learning things like how to give a good public speech.

Ms. Goodrum recognized that the way you inspire others is to expand their view of the world and then reinforce in them a belief that they can explore that world. She could see there was a light inside of me that longed to shine in some way that I could not yet envision, so she helped feed my imagination. And the more she invested, the more she saw the light get brighter and brighter because—and this is an important key—I was open to the lessons she could teach me.

My expectations also were shaped by Ernie Cline, the high school basketball coach at Arsenal Tech. Coach Cline, who played at Arsenal before going to Butler University, is in the Indiana Basketball Hall of Fame, which, if you know anything about basketball, is a really big deal. He not only was a great player, but he won a school record 183 games at Arsenal and coached high school All-Americans like two of my peers, Antonio Martin and Landon Turner.

I was not among the All-Americans he coached. In fact, I wasn't a good enough player to make the team. But Coach Cline wasn't just interested in the All-Americans who could help him win games and earn him a spot in the state's basketball hall of fame. He wanted to be a hall of fame leader by having a positive impact on as many students as he could.

Coach Cline recognized something of value in me and made investments that shaped my expectations for the future. For instance, he gave me responsibilities as the team's manager—not just washing towels and uniforms, but bigger duties like making hotel arrangements or planning where the team would eat when we traveled. He trusted me with things that mattered, and my confidence grew that I was capable of making good decisions and getting things done.

People like Coach Cline and Ms. Goodrum opened my heart and mind to new possibilities that I eagerly embraced. They chose to see the best in me, and they helped me see the best in myself. More than that, they helped me see the best in other people, especially in terms of race. Their examples reinforced what my mother lived and taught— that I could go through life without seeing everything and everyone through the lens of skin tones.

Before long, a cyclical process took place where positive beliefs began to feed positive beliefs. Others believed in me, which fed my belief in myself, which led others to believe in me even more, which strengthened my self-belief. As a result, I didn't limit myself with beliefs about what I couldn't be or what I had to be, and that gave power and meaning to everything else I believed.

For me, in fact, expectations represented freedom. But they easily could have been my prison.

BUILDING OUR BASTILLE

The unfortunate reality is that expectations often form holding cells that might as well be made of steel bars, stone walls, and iron chains.

For starters, there are the lofty expectations we can't or perhaps don't want to live up to. These steel bars surround us and seem to shrink in on us the longer we are held within them. Next, there are the negative expectations we believe and adopt for ourselves. These are the stone walls that hold us back from seeing, much less experiencing, our full potential. And, finally, there are the expectations that get crushed by our personal failures. These are the chains of unforgiveness.

All of these forms of expectations contributed to the exhaustion of my personal experience, but an uncompromising mindset helped keep me out of jail (figuratively speaking, of course).

Steel bars.

It's amazing how differently we can see an expectation depending on how it's presented to us or how it naturally fits with us. If we come up with the idea or feel good about it, the lofty expectation motivates and inspires us. But if it's forced on us or feels unnatural, we begin to suffocate within a prison cell that feels like it holds no oxygen.

There's an old saying that's often used in twelve-step recovery programs that goes like this: "Expectations are premeditated resentments." When we feel saddled with expectations that are unrealistic, that don't include the support we need to achieve our goals, or that don't align with who we are or what we want in life, then the seeds of resentment begin to take root, not only in us but in those around us.

This is often why kids turn to drugs or rebel against their parents—they resent something about the expectations that are placed on them. I've had friends and coworkers who felt pressure to live up to an older sibling's success. Or they resented being asked to pay the price it would take to achieve something that was really their parent's dream and not their own—like to be a doctor or a professional athlete or whatever.

When someone tells us that we *should* do something or be something, we don't own the vision in the same way as when we tell *ourselves* that we should do something or be something. True vision-casting leaders like Ms. Goodrum and Coach Cline help us discover and embrace higher expectations, and then they support us, sometimes in challenging ways, and encourage us as we pursue them.

Stone walls.

In other cases, expectations become prisons because they trap us behind the bars of our negative beliefs. We buy into a lie, and the lie eventually defines us.

One of the biggest reasons that racism remains such a prevalent pattern in America is that so many children are still led to believe they are inferior—or taught that they are superior. Those who believe they are inferior to others are imprisoned by a false limitation; those who believe they are superior to others are imprisoned by ignorance. Either way, they are given an expectation, and it imprisons them for as long as they let it.

There were many times growing up when adults projected an expectation of inferiority in my direction. Sometimes it was clearly intentional; other times it was subtle or even inadvertent. Maybe it was the teacher who never called on me in class or the store clerk who watched me with a suspicious glare as I shopped. Fortunately for me, I had other voices—my mother, Coach Cline, Ms. Goodrum, for instance—who counterbalanced the negative and helped me see my potential.

Iron chains.

Finally, our expectations become a prison when we don't respond well to failure. I call this the chains of unforgiveness.

When I was sixteen, for instance, I was alone in a grocery store on a winter afternoon when, for no good reason, I stuck something insignificant in my coat and walked out the door without paying. Someone saw me, of course, and yelled for me to stop, which prompted me to run.

In my mind, I would use my blazing speed to race across the street and disappear down some back alley. In reality, an employee grabbed me before I could get out of the parking lot. Soon I found myself wearing handcuffs in a small office with the white store manager and a white police officer—every African American teenager's dream, right?

There was no denying my guilt, but now I had to make some decisions about how I would respond to that guilt. Would I say nothing? Would I lie? Would I blame others? Would I try to justify my actions? Would I lash out?

Now, Momma had raised me not to lie or steal, and I already had broken one of those commandments. I wasn't about to break another. So I begged for mercy. Maybe someone put in a good word for me without me knowing it, but I suspect my freedom hinged on a key fear that I shared while making my plea—I had no desire to face a judge or go to jail, I told them, but I was far more concerned about facing the five-foot, four-inch-tall Lanie Mae White! I promised to never steal again if they would let me go and never tell my mother. They complied on both counts.

Later, I realized it was a crossroads moment. I could have become addicted to the adrenaline rush of stealing. I could have become emboldened by my ability to talk my way out of a jam. I could have bought in to negative expectations that had been reinforced about my character and my future.

Thankfully, I made the right choice and recommitted to values like honesty and integrity. I upheld my promise to never steal again, and I moved forward in pursuit of a better life.

To do that, however, I had to forgive myself for not living up to the expectations my mother had set for me and that I had embraced for myself.

I could have dismissed my mistake as irrelevant and walked away without learning anything from it. I also could have justified it with some excuse. And I could have convinced myself that I somehow deserved the second chance the officer and store manager gave me. But none of that would release me from my guilt. Instead, I had to own my mistake without letting it own me.

FINDING FREEDOM

Expectations don't have to be a prison. They actually can free you when you discover that you are allowed to define and redefine them based on your uncompromising values.

When I sat on a battered old couch in Georgia in the spring of 1971 eavesdropping on adult family members as they told my mother her three boys would never amount to anything, I had little reason not to believe them. Instead, their negative expectations became our motivation. My mother was determined to prove them wrong, and so was I.

There are many reasons, of course, why life has turned out well for me. The biggest, I believe, is because I had a praying mother and, later, a praying wife. But I also understand that I had to take action on the opportunities Providence provided. When He placed people in my life who believed in me and helped me redefine the expectations I had for my life, I had to buy in and then do the work to make those expectations a reality.

The first part of that equation—buying in—speaks to the very heart of how expectations become something that free us rather than something that hold us back. Later, I'll talk about the importance of focusing on two things we truly can control—our attitude and our effort. But both of those are controlled by what we think, and I firmly believe that if you are in control of what's in your head, your expectations can be as big as you want them to be.

When we're young, we might blindly embrace every idea an authority figure shares with us. As we grow older, however, we're responsible for vetting what we allow into our minds. We decide what movies we will watch, what songs we will put on our playlist, or what people we will spend time with. And we decide if we'll believe someone who tells us we can't do this or we have to do that. This is no small matter, because what we decide about what we allow into our minds shapes our vision of what the future can be.

As leaders, however, we're not only responsible for owning our expectations but for cultivating positive expectations in everyone around us.

I was at Harvard for some training a few years back when I came up with a way to nurture some positive expectations for my son. I dropped into a store one afternoon and purchased several Harvard sweatshirts for him—all of different sizes. That way, as he grew out of one, he could slip into another. Stevie is nine years old right now, and guess what he says when I ask him where he's going to college?

"Dad," he says, "I'm moving to Boston, and I'm going to Harvard."

Then he adds, "When I go, does that mean I can be a Celtics and Red Sox fan?"

And, of course, I say, "No. We don't like them."

I'm joking. Sort of. But whether he goes to Harvard (or goes to the dark side by embracing Boston's sports teams) is not the point. The point is that he sees top colleges as realistic expectations. As he gets older and refines the hopes and dreams for his life, we'll support him and do our best to make sure he has the resources to achieve his goals. And hopefully he will define them with a positive mindset and a high degree of self-confidence.

When it comes to expectations, we free ourselves and others by constantly finding positive ways to remind ourselves and them about those expectations. We need them to soak into us and become part of who we are.

I've found that if we keep our goals top of mind, we are inspired to attack them in different ways. Maybe we write them on a wall or create some other symbol that reminds us of our dreams. It doesn't matter if it's a goal about losing weight, buying a dream car, going to a prestigious college, or achieving a career milestone—filling our minds consistently with the right expectations frees us to make it a reality.

EXPECTATIONS TO ACTIONS

When someone asks me for career advice, I typically begin my response with a question: *What are your hopes and dreams?* I want to understand the expectations they've set for themselves and why those expectations matter.

In cases where it's clear that they undervalue their abilities and their potential, I might challenge them to aspire to something bigger. How I would do that depends on the relationship, but the idea is to help them see what's available that they might be missing so they can make a more informed choice. It's not my role, however, to tell someone where they should live, what job they should take, who they should date, or anything else about how they should live their life. Few things smell worse than a big pile of "should." But one role of a leader is to help people see their options, let them know you believe in them, and show them love by supporting them in whatever positive path they choose.

Here's a glimpse into how this worked in my career.

At some point along the way, I decided I wanted to be the CEO of a public company. But like almost everything else in my professional career, I knew I had to win that job. How did I know? Because one of my coaches set that expectation for me.

Some people are "groomed" for certain roles, he told me. *It's theirs to lose. That's not the case for you. But the jobs you want are yours to win. You have to go win them.*

Everything about growing up black in America told me this was true. The world wasn't handing out CEO jobs to African Americans. I could see that easily enough, but the statistics backed it up.

The US Bureau of Labor Statistics reports that African Americans, Asians, and Hispanics make up more than 36 percent of the workforce but just 16 percent of the chief executives. Just 4.1 percent of chief executives are African Americans, who make up 12.3 percent of the workforce.[7] In large public companies, the numbers are even worse. There have only been fifteen black CEOs of Fortune 500 companies since 1955, and, as of 2019, there were only four (all men).[8]

If I was going to "win" the job I wanted, I knew I had to meet, and in some cases exceed, the expectations others would have for me so I could prove to them I was the right person for each promotion. I had two significant revelations along the way. One, I needed to stay close to the profit and loss statement (P&L). And, two, I needed to prove I could lead large groups of people.

When you double-click on the management and professional occupations, you realize most of the people of color are in jobs like human resources, diversity, corporate social responsibility, or other functional roles. Those jobs are important, but they typically aren't found on the road to the C-suite. A study by the consulting firm Korn Ferry found that fewer than 10 percent of Fortune 500 leaders in P&L roles were black,[9] and as someone once told me, if you want to advance to the top of a public company, you need to stay near the P&L.

---

7   "Employed persons by detailed occupation, sex, race, and Hispanic or Latino ethnicity," US Bureau of Labor Statistics, *https://www.bls.gov/cps/cpsaat11.htm,* last accessed May 27, 2020.

8   "Korn Ferry Study Reveals United States Black P&L Leaders are Some of the Highest Performing Executives in the U.S. C-Suite," Korn Ferry, October 10, 2019, *https://www.kornferry.com/about-us/press/korn-ferry-study-reveals-united-states-black-pl-leaders-are-some-of-the-highest-performing-executives-in-the-us-c-suite,* last accessed May 27, 2020.

9   "The Black P&L Leader: Insights and Lessons from Senior Black P&L Leaders in Corporate America," Korn Ferry and the Executive Leadership Council, 2019, https://infokf.kornferry.com/The-Black-PandL-Leader-Report.html, last accessed May 27, 2020.

There are at least three reasons why this is important. One, the P&L is all about the numbers, and the numbers are clear and measurable. There's no subjectivity, so you're less likely to get passed over strictly because of someone's opinion. That still happens, and it has happened to me, but you're either hitting the numbers or you're not, so at least you have those facts to support your case. Two, the best way to demonstrate your value is by helping the company make money. And, three, the other people involved with the P&L are at the center of the company. That's where decisions are made.

So throughout my career, I've tried to make sure I stayed close to sales or something that was generating cash or results because it was easy to measure, generated value for the company, and put me in contact with the decision-makers.

The second revelation is what brought me into the cable business. I started out in medical sales, then worked for Pepsi, and then Colgate-Palmolive. I worked for great companies and great people, and I enjoyed my work. And by 1996, I was confident that I had what it took to lead a public company. I had received encouragement from people I respected, and I had a track record of success. I embraced that expectation.

About that time, I got a call from a headhunter suggesting I consider a job in the cable industry. I was running the North American toothbrush business for Colgate-Palmolive, which was a very good job, but I knew that my next step if I wanted to keep going up the ladder there was to take an international assignment, and I wasn't very interested in that. The headhunter pointed out another issue I faced. In my current role, only about thirty people reported to me. Even if I took an international assignment with Colgate-Palmolive, that number would only grow to about three hundred. But if I moved to the cable industry, I would be responsible for about three thousand people.

"The single biggest attribute needed to be CEO," she told me, "is the ability to motivate large groups of men and women. You can get that experience in the cable industry, and it will better position you to move up even if you eventually go to some other company in some other industry."

There's more than one path to the top of the corporate ladder, but that one worked well for me. For several reasons, I didn't become CEO of a public company. But, thanks to sponsorships by leaders such as Brian Roberts, Steve Burke, and Dave Watson, I did become president of Comcast West. There I was responsible for a workforce that was thirty thousand people strong. As a stand-alone company, it would have been a Fortune 150 enterprise. So while the expectations I had for myself didn't land me the title of CEO, they did help me land the results I wanted, and that was even more valuable than the title.

What mattered even more, however, was how I pursued my expectations. That's where the seven pathways came into play. Knowing where I was going and believing I could get there were valuable because they helped define the destination. A fiercely independent, radically responsible, scrappy, and undistracted mindset with an unwavering commitment to the seven pathways helped ensure that I not only got there, but I got there the right way.

In fact, until I got on the first pathway and shifted the motives that were driving me toward my expectations, I had very little chance of achieving a life worth living. To find real success, I had to find my fight.

Chapter 3

Pathway 1—Find Your Fight

Identifying your why gives you meaning and direction.

THE CAR IN MY DRIVEWAY was a 1982 BMW—a convertible in the 318 series. Black on black. Leather seats. All the bells. All the whistles. She was freshly washed and waxed, as always, and she was shining in the late afternoon sun like the perfect symbol of success.

I'm telling you, that was *the car* to own. And best of all, I owned it. Well, me and the credit union. Same with the home at the end of the driveway. The house and the mortgage belonged to me.

I sat quietly in the driver's seat of that BMW on a chilly day in spring 1986, the engine idling gently under the hood as I contemplated my next move.

Go inside? I thought. *And then what?*

A million memories flooded my thoughts, but the most persistent was the one from earlier in the day, an unanticipated left hook from my boss that sent me to my knees and took my career down with me. He didn't hit me with his fist, of course. It was worse than that. Much worse. He hit me with his words.

You are fired, he said.

How could this be? I kept thinking. *How could he fire me?*

Yet, that's exactly what he did. He called me up and said he was flying to Michigan for a visit. He was fairly new to the role as my supervisor, so I figured I was getting a pep talk, maybe some advice on how to jump-start my team to a better year than we'd had in 1985. Perhaps even another promotion. But there was no pep in his talk and definitely no promotion.

I can't recall exactly what he said, but I'll never forget the gist of it.

This is not working out.... You're not adding value, and you're not a good fit.... You're being relieved of your duties.... You are fired.

There was no easing me gently into my new reality. His voice was about as comforting as a two-by-four to the bridge of my nose.

Little did I know it, but it was finally time for me to find my fight.

FINDING MY FIGHT

The foundations for success in my early life were laid by encouraging people like my mother, my teachers, and mentors like my uncles and Coach Cline; but I had to get knocked down to find my fight. Once I found it, however, everything changed for one simple reason: my success became others-focused rather than self-focused.

Your fight is what brings virtue, energy, and direction to your purpose for going through life—it's what gives your why meaning. When we find our fight, it becomes one and the same with our why, and it changes our mindset and approach as we pursue our purpose. Exhaustion and other obstacles don't stand a chance. Meaningful success follows, as long as we never relinquish the power that comes from an unwavering commitment to why we exist.

For years, my why was all about escaping poverty, making money, and earning the trappings of corporate success. I knew all about setting goals and chasing my dreams, and I achieved most of the results I wanted. My goals and dreams weren't necessarily bad, but they also weren't particularly honorable. In fact, most of what I was chasing wasn't truly worth fighting for because it centered around just one person—me.

Somewhere deep inside, I knew my why shouldn't be anchored to things that were so superficial. There had to be more to life than chasing the next promotion and a bigger paycheck. There was no contentment in achieving things that were so difficult to earn but so easy to lose. I had to find a deeper purpose that motivated me to get up, to get going, to never quit, to battle like crazy to make it happen, and to find satisfaction in knowing that I had fought for it, regardless of the result. It had to be about something that was bigger than myself.

I saw that type of fight in my mother, but I didn't fully connect all the dots when I was growing up or even as a young adult. Later, I realized the strength she found in finding her personal fight and the power I could tap into by finding mine.

My mother's lifelong dream had nothing to do with cleaning rooms in a cheap motel or being a janitor at a public school. There's no dishonor in those jobs, but a passion for that type of work wasn't the motivating factor that kept her going when life seemed unfair and the demands seemed unrelenting.

Like all of us, she needed to connect her work to something deeper, something worth fighting for. She linked it to her vision for her sons—to making sure my brothers and I embraced the values we needed for success in our careers and in our families.

That's why we had rules that were very different from so many other families where I grew up. We had to be home before the streetlights came on, and we weren't allowed to go to the store alone, for instance, because those were ways she could help protect us from some of the violence common around our neighborhood. That's why she worked so hard—to give us a chance in life. She had a dream for us, and she knew that making it a reality required her to live and lead differently from the norm.

Creating a stable future for her sons was the source of her power, and she wasn't willing to give that up. She fought for it daily, sometimes from minute to minute. It kept her going when relatives said, "Those kids won't amount to anything." And when the days grew long and the work felt unbearable, she tapped into that power by reminding herself what was at stake.

A friend of mine once asked my mother what gave her the courage to leave Georgia and fight through so many challenges that came our way in Indiana. "My whole life," Momma said with tears pooling in her eyes, "my whole heart was on my sons. That's who I was concerned about. I didn't want to leave my mom. But I knew it would be best for my boys."

Momma had found her fight, and no one could take it from her.

My fight emerged over time and involves creating an environment where others can succeed—a table of prosperity where everyone can participate and enjoy life. But the key moment in developing my fight occurred in 1986 when I was fired.

To that point, I had operated with many of the values that are key to success, and success had followed. I did what I was told by people I respected, studied hard, put in long hours, and got positive results from the blood and sweat I was pouring into my efforts. That got me through high school and college, and it was a great formula for launching my professional career.

I joined the sales team of American Converters, a division of American Hospital Supply, on June 21, 1982, shortly after graduating from Indiana University. My first stop was Chicago, where around twenty-five recent college grads went through training before the company sent us off in different directions, each of us intent on becoming the fastest horse in the race to win fame and fortune.

They placed me in the Northeast. I lived in New Jersey and sold disposable drapes and gowns to hospital surgical units in the tristate area. I had great mentors in men like Scott Murphy, Bob Normyle, and Ross Clark—veterans who took me under their wings and taught me the ropes when it came to selling medical supplies. And in 1983, my first full year, I was the top quota breaker in the company, beating my target by 54 percent.

I went to the company's annual convention in spring 1984 in a double-breasted pinstriped suit, with a freshly pressed white shirt, a red power tie, and sparkling black shoes—all my treat to myself thanks to the $27,000 I had earned in salary and commissions. And I proudly wore that suit as I accepted two awards, one for smashing that quota like a rock going through a plate-glass window and the other for being named the 1983 Rookie of the Year.

By March 1984, the company moved me to Chicago as a director of product management. I spent a few months helping develop new products and traveling to our plant in Mexico before a restructuring landed me another promotion. Now I was off to Ann Arbor, Michigan, as a regional sales manager, the youngest in the company to hold that title.

As a Hoosier, I was not a fan of the maize and blue (the University of Michigan's colors), but college rivalries aside, it was a great place to live. I was young, so the college vibe fit me well. And since I was now making a cool $44,000 a year, I figured it was time to buy a house and a car. Might as well make the car a BMW, right?

The house sat at the end of a cul-de-sac and came with a $100,000 price tag. It was framed in red brick and had five bedrooms, four baths, a two-car garage, and a screened porch. My mother, uncle, aunt, and brothers all drove up from Indianapolis and stayed several days with me shortly after I moved in, and it was hard not to bask in the limelight. I was the first in our family to graduate from a university, and I had a great job, a nice house, a trendy car, and a momma who was the envy of all her church-lady friends.

Privately, however, I had my doubts and fears. This had all happened fast, and at times I felt like an impostor. *Have I really earned this? Do I deserve it? Surely someone will wise up before long and burst the bubble. But until they do, I'll fake it until I make it.*

In retrospect, it became clear that I had a lot to learn about leading people. I had been given assignments and responsibilities throughout my life, as well as the structure and resources to get them done. And I had found personal success early in my career by taking care of my supervisors and winning business for the company. Those assignments typically had one thing in common: I was responsible for my results, not the results of others. So when I arrived at Ann Arbor, I wasn't fully prepared to lead a team.

When I became the supervisor, I figured I was the big cheese and my ten direct reports would go to work making me look good. They didn't, and who could blame them? I didn't show them the way or give them the support they needed to do their best work.

In 1985, my first full year as a "leader" in Michigan, there were thirty regional sales teams in the company, and my team finished, drumroll, please—number thirty. I'll never forget walking through the convention center after the awards banquet for that year. Someone from another regional team yelled for us to wait on him, and one of my sales guys summed up the feeling of our team.

"You don't want to walk with us," he said. "We're dead last."

My team had been looking for a leader to help them figure things out, and I had been living on my past successes. I didn't understand that the most fundamental aspect of leadership is serving others.

And that is why I was fired.

EMBRACING MY FIGHT (THREE WORDS)

When I finally got out of my car and walked into my home on the day I was fired, I had no idea what the future would hold for me. I dreaded telling my friends. And I dreaded telling my family. So, of course, I told no one.

I felt embarrassed. Exposed. Alone. Defeated.

Most of all, I felt exhausted.

And while I knew I wasn't getting the results I wanted or that the company wanted, I also couldn't help feeling like I wasn't given a chance at success. I wasn't given a warning. I wasn't given any coaching—no training and development to help me succeed, no mentoring, no plan to help me improve my areas of weakness. I wasn't given time to course correct.

There wasn't an emphasis on training and development for anyone back then, but it wasn't always a true meritocracy. It felt unfair, and it was impossible for me not to wonder if my white boss was treating me differently than he would have treated someone who was white. I was fired by an older white man who worked with older white men, and I have no doubt that they didn't understand me as a person because our backgrounds were dramatically different.

This was and still is a common dilemma for many black Americans in the corporate world. We know racism exists. Sometimes it's intentional, while other times it's born of unconscious bias. Sometimes it's easy to spot, other times it's not. We realize that racism isn't the cause of every bad thing that happens in our lives, but the suspicion—not being sure—feeds the fear that one wrong move will doom our future by providing someone with a reason to get rid of us.

Many of us use that fear as a motivation to work harder, dress sharper, and prepare better than everyone else. We realize we must make an uncompromising commitment to excellence in our work—and to getting up regardless of whether we were knocked down or fell on our own.

Still, there's a tension that comes in life when you feel like you always need to look over your shoulder while racing up a stairway made of eggshells. Eventually, you know something will break and you will fall, and that's when you wonder, as I wondered in 1986, if anyone remembers anything you'd ever done right.

No matter how I looked at it, though, I couldn't stop blaming myself. I could cry foul all day long, but I knew I had failed. Sports coaches like to say that the film doesn't lie, and our version of the film showed that my team wasn't getting good results. That was the bottom line.

Maybe I was never good enough to begin with, I thought.

I wanted to crawl in a hole and hide from the world. I had never lived in the same room with failure, and I wasn't sure how to treat him. But he wouldn't go away. He just sat there laughing and saying, *I told you so!*

Then the phone rang.

"How you doing, man?"

It was Darnell Martin. He was a vice president in the distribution division of American Hospital Supply. I was in a products division, so he wasn't involved in the decision to let me go. But as an older, high-ranking African American leader in the company, he had taken an outsider's interest in my career and had learned through corporate channels that I had been released.

"How you think I'm doing?" I said, still frustrated and hurt. "I just got fired!"

The next words from his mouth, however, changed everything.

"I got you," he said.

At first, I thought he was just providing words of encouragement, but it turned out that he was offering much, much more. He wasn't just offering empathy, sympathy, or even a letter of recommendation once I had dusted off my résumé and jumped back into the job market. He was offering an opportunity—an opportunity to learn and grow.

Three words had knocked me down: *You are fired.*

Now three words were lifting me up: *I got you.*

"I believe there's more in you," Darnell said. "I don't know what I have available, but if you're interested, I'm going to grab you by the shoulder and I'm going to move you to Chicago. Same salary. You're going to work in my operation in a temporary position, and we're going to figure this out for the long term."

Of course, I nearly jumped through the phone to accept his offer. And he was true to his word. I spent six months in Chicago, then moved to Connecticut as a regional manager.

Very few people ever knew I'd been fired, because I certainly wasn't eager to share that detail. I let everyone think it was just another promotion, a natural progression in my career. (It was nearly thirty years later when I let it slip in a phone call with my mother. "Let you go?" she said with shock in her voice. "What do you mean, '*Let you go?!*'")

But while others were in the dark about my setback, I knew. And I wasn't about to waste the opportunity—especially when I also knew how rare such second chances were for black men in the corporate world.

It was during those six months in Chicago that I began to find my fight.

I discovered during that short period of my life that when you are sailing along on a golden highway and you suddenly get knocked into a muddy ditch, you get back on the road with a fresh awareness about your surroundings. That was my experience, anyway. I knew I needed to change, and I was watching and learning, searching for what I could see in others who were successful leaders that might have been missing in me.

What I saw in Darnell and Gary (my new boss) were leaders who took care of the people they led, and that's what I was missing.

For starters, I learned from Darnell's example. Helping me wasn't a self-serving move on his part. In fact, it might have cost him in the eyes of some other leaders. He also didn't have what we in the black community sometimes refer to as a "crabs in a bucket" mentality—a fear of helping out someone because it might cost you the rare available leadership position. Instead, he was willing to take a chance, be authentic, and serve selflessly simply because he believed in me and saw it as the right thing to do.

He took a huge chance on me, and I did not want to let him down.

I also learned from the job he provided. I had a new boss who was supportive and helpful. I had effectively been dumped into his lap, but he respected and trusted Darnell—because Darnell had supported him and earned that respect and trust.

Like Darnell, Gary taught by example what it looked like to serve others, but I also had to put those lessons into action. I had no supervisory responsibilities in this job, and I had no quotas to hit. Instead, I was an individual contributor working on special projects, but my success was tied to my ability to work with other people in a collaborative fashion. The more I learned to serve the team around me, the more I learned what it meant to really lead.

An uncompromising mindset about this approach to leadership became the basis of my fight.

LIVING MY FIGHT

My why had always been about making money and get-ting to the top of the food chain. My entire self-esteem had been tied up in how much I made, how successful I was, and what other people thought of me. I wanted to become the CEO of a public company, for instance, because that title would validate my professional success and my worth as a person.

When I got fired, my mindset began to shift. I still wanted to become a CEO, but for a different reason—I came to see it as a platform for reaching and helping hun-dreds and hundreds of men and women. The title became less important, because the fight was what mattered. And I didn't have to become a CEO to live out an uncom-promising commitment to my fight. I could do it wher-ever I was and with whatever title happened to be on my business card.

In 1987, for instance, not long after my career got back on track thanks to the hand up from Darnell, a headhunter approached me about a job with Pepsi. It was a great chance to gain experience in a different industry and with a hip company that was well known and growing. I knew I couldn't pass it up. When I talked to the headhunter, how-ever, I didn't just focus on what Pepsi could do for me. I told him about three other black leaders I knew who also would be fantastic hires. All three of them ended up land-ing jobs that helped advance their careers.

Although I was doing fine at American Hospital Supply, Pepsi offered opportunities that could accelerate my career. There were just more ladders that could get me closer to the top. And the higher I rose in organizations, the more people I could gather around that table of prosperity. Eventually, as president of Comcast West, I was reaching more than thirty thousand employees. My dream had stayed the same, but the all-important motive behind it—my why, my fight—had changed. And that made the achievements that came along the way truly meaningful.

I've had plenty more selfish moments, of course, and I continued to learn lessons about how to lead, but I no longer struggled with my why. I had found a worthy fight, and I became determined to tap into that power with an uncompromising commitment.

Sometimes this showed up in policies and decisions that were easily seen and measured. For instance, when I was president of Comcast West, we were able to create the Linked to Leadership program—L2L—as a means of identifying and training frontline hourly workers who demonstrated leadership potential. Each year, two hundred people graduated from L2L, which means we helped grow two thousand leaders in the first ten years.

A high percentage of our frontline workers are minorities, so I felt like this program helped encourage many of them to fight through whatever forms of exhaustion they had experienced. And because 70 percent of the graduates advanced into leadership positions across the US with Comcast, I know it helped increase the diversity in our leadership ranks while also having an immeasurable impact on their families.

At other times, my efforts to live out my fight were more personal. I spent a great deal of time asking questions and then listening to the people on my team share things that were important to them, not just about the challenges they were facing in work but their hopes and dreams and struggles in life. Getting to know people at a deeper level was the only way I could use whatever wisdom and influence I had gained to support them in their personal journey. It positioned me to give them the same type of hand up that I had been given, which allowed me to share in their success.

Some of my proudest moments as president of Comcast West, in fact, came when people around me were promoted—people like Rich Jennings. I always made a point to look across the company with an eye toward talent, knowing that, at the very least, I could play a role in encouraging those emerging leaders, and that at some point, they might end up working with me or for me. I had followed Rich's career as he advanced in another division of Comcast, knew his potential, and jumped when the chance came to add him to my team in 2011.

As we worked together, I learned more and more about his wife, his three daughters, his goals for their lives, and the things he hoped to accomplish professionally. For instance, he often talked about going to Notre Dame, about how he worked as a disc jockey to help pay his way through school, about what was going on in the lives of his daughters, and about his personal career aspirations.

I did my best to take him under my wing, especially when it came to his career. That meant giving him opportunities to prove himself with high-impact projects, supporting him even at times when he struggled, and giving him feedback to help him grow toward his goals. It also included more subtle advice like how to carry himself as a leader.

I remember one time when Rich joined me for a community event sponsored by Comcast. The mayor of Denver was there, and our role was to represent the company during the formal parts of the event as well as informally as we interacted with community leaders and other volunteers. It was a Saturday, so I wasn't wearing a suit, but I was still well dressed—nice jeans, a stylish collared shirt, and dress shoes. Rich, who is about ten years my junior, showed up far more casually. He still looked sharp, mind you, but this wasn't a hip-hop event. His pants were tucked into his boots, and he was wearing a knit cap on his head.

My advice to him was something like this: *It's fine to express your authentic self in the way you dress, but that's not the look of a senior vice president. Your appearance sends a message, and you want people to pick you out as a leader who commands attention and respect.*

Every company is different when it comes to things like dress, but I knew this: black leaders who want to advance in large corporate organizations need to look the part if they want to get the part. Performance matters, but so do perceptions. You don't have to like that reality, but you can't deny it.

One of the ways Rich knew I was truly vested in his career was by the quality of my feedback. It's easy to tell people what they want to hear. It's harder, but much more meaningful, to tell people what they need to hear in encouraging ways that help them grow.

The thing about Rich is that he never took offense to the advice or direction I gave him, even if he didn't always agree with me or if it was something that forced him out of his comfort zones. Instead, he soaked it in and learned from it. And the reward for me came as he continually embraced the coaching and earned more and more responsibility that led to his future success.

Imagine the pride I felt, given our shared history, when Rich was approved to replace me as president of Comcast West. He earned that opportunity, not me, but I took great joy in making sure he had a place at the table, because that is what my fight is all about.

How I have lived out my fight has evolved over time, because I have grown as a person and as a leader, and because my roles and responsibilities have changed. I eventually connected it to my faith, which for years was hollow and lifeless. And I've found new and more meaning-ful ways to make it a part of my marriage, how I participate in raising our son, and how I serve others outside of my work environment. Regardless of the area of my life or the work that I'm doing, however, my uncompromising com-mitment to my fight guides my decisions and my actions.

YOUR PERSONAL FIGHT

Before you can truly move forward toward a meaningful journey, I believe you have to pause and identify what's worth fighting for in your life. And then you have to fight for it every day. Here are a few lessons I learned along the way that might help you find a why that's worth fighting for in an uncompromising fashion:

Wake up.

In May 1962, the novelist William Melvin Kelley wrote an article for *The New York Times* titled, "If You're Woke You Dig It." It wasn't the first literary reference to "woke," but it probably had more to do than anything else with propel-ling the term into the mainstream culture.

It's experienced a revival in recent years, mostly in rela-tionship to social justice issues. Some see it as inspirational and positive, others as divisive and negative. For me, the heart of the meaning is this: We all need a deep sense of awareness—to wake up to the realities in us and around us. So I'm not challenging you to wake up to my view of the world; I'm challenging you to wake up to the truth about who you are and what's going on in your world so you can figure out what really matters to you.

That type of "wokeness" is essential in finding a worthy fight.

The self-awareness part begins by regularly taking an objective look at yourself. Personally, I've never had an out-of-body experience. But I've found that part of staying woke involves stepping out of myself (mentally), pausing, and taking inventory of who I am—things like my strengths, my weaknesses, and my passions—and where I'm going.

This healthy habit of regular self-evaluation needs to be supplemented by objective outside opinions. For some, a strengths, personality, or motivations assessment is helpful. And a 360-degree assessment can help us see the gaps between how we see ourselves and how others see us. It also helps to talk through these issues with our trusted advisors like a spouse, mentors, or close friends.

Developing a well of self-awareness ensures we won't miss the signs that are pointing us toward our fight. It helps us say something like, *These are my strengths and these are the activities that make me feel most alive and at my best. I'm going to define a fight that allows me to spend most of my time using those strengths and doing those activities.*

But we also need a wokeness about the realities and opportunities around us, because that will help us define and refine the fight that's within us.

Getting fired, for instance, would not have led me to my fight if I hadn't been awake enough to recognize the gift that was wrapped in those exit papers.

I have found that opportunities sometimes come when we're napping; by the time we get off the couch, they're gone. Or maybe they come while we're complaining and blaming. Or while we're busy telling the world about all of our accomplishments. Or when we simply don't take the time to look up from the hustle and bustle of our lives to see what's going on.

When we're not intentional and proactive about staying alert to opportunities, we're often left with regrets about what might have been. I've missed many opportunities through the years, but I have an uncompromising commitment not to miss the next one. Without that commitment, I might as well take a nap on the sofa.

Never relinquish your power.

I once worked with a guy, I'll call him Gus, who hated his job, knew he hated his job, and told me he hated his job. He looked miserable, acted miserable, and made everyone around him miserable.

Why did he stay in that role? Because he felt trapped by his stuff. He had two big car payments, a mortgage on a large home, a boat, and the latest and greatest gadgets the tech world could offer. He was determined to get his two kids into an expensive private college, and he had a side hustle as part owner of a local retail store. It was a fragile house of cards, and he was afraid he'd lose his possessions if he left his miserable job.

This guy never got out there and found his real fight. And as a result, he relinquished his power, because his power—his *real* power—could only be found in a why that was worth fighting to achieve.

Finding meaning in things like making money, getting promotions, earning accolades, buying more stuff, or pleasing people can cause us to fight for something that ends up owning us rather than us owning our fight. We effectively give up our power to live a meaningful life to something or someone else.

Once I was exposed to what life could look like if I had money in my pockets, I flat-out never wanted to be poor again. It became a huge motivator—something I still consider a "good fear." I wanted to own my own home, and I set goals of earning $100,000 a year by the time I was thirty and of becoming CEO of a public company. There was nothing wrong with those types of ambitions, but I've found they can become our master unless they're put in the proper perspective.

If you have no why or if you are ruled by the wrong why, then you risk slipping easily into a pattern where you submit to people and circumstances that aren't always in your best interest. If you let a supervisor treat you with total disdain, for instance, you have relinquished your power and given it to that supervisor. He or she can control you, and very often that will be the case. You'll end up working ridiculous hours and getting treated like crap.

If, on the other hand, you figure out what in life is really worth fighting for, it provides fuel for your journey, especially in tough times or when you get slightly off track. You might have to endure a year or two in a bad situation, but you can mentally plan your exit strategy and work toward goals that are connected to your fight. You won't always have control over the circumstances, but in your heart and mind you will know that you have the power to keep fighting for what really matters to you.

For me, a key to never relinquishing my power was to never view myself as a victim. Getting fired was a crossroads moment, one of a dozen or so when how I chose to respond would have a huge impact on my future. Those moments often included the option of viewing myself as either a victor or a victim.

I'm sure it helped that I got a call so soon with another opportunity, but I didn't waste much time focusing on the unfair aspects of my firing. It wasn't going to change my situation, and seeing myself as a victim would have given them a power over me. I wasn't willing to give them that power.

It also would have denied me the opportunity to look in the mirror and learn from the mistakes I needed to own. Victims seldom own their mistakes, because they're too busy casting out blame. I wasn't yet victorious, but I was determined to own my mistakes, learn from them, and move forward with the mindset of a victor.

I recognize that I had many opportunities that others didn't have growing up. I had a mother who loved me, who kept me safe, who kept me fed, who provided discipline, and who encouraged me to succeed in every area of life. You might have had it much worse than me. No matter how bad you've had it, though, you, too, have opportunities to succeed. If you choose to never relinquish your fight, you can discover your why and pursue it in uncompromising fashion.

Find purpose in your fires.

In a related way, I believe it's hard to find our fight without tapping into our struggles and failures. These are the fires that help us define, test, and refine our fight so that we know it's real. It's one thing to say we will fight for something. It's another to actually jump into the fray when things get hard or we get knocked down, especially if we have the option of walking away.

Vernon Jordan, for instance, found purpose in the fires he experienced in the 1950s. As a college student, Jordan spent a few summers working as a waiter and chauffeur for Robert F. Maddox, who was a successful banker, former mayor of Atlanta, and member of the Old South aristocracy.

Maddox, who was in his eighties at the time, once was surprised to find Jordan in his library reading a book. He had no idea that Jordan could read, much less that he was a college student at the otherwise all-white DePauw University in Indiana.

That night at dinner, as Jordan served soup to Maddox, his children, and their spouses, Maddox said he had an announcement to make: "Vernon can read," he said. And the next day, he felt compelled to share this astonishing news with two of his friends as Jordan stood nearby.

Those three words became the title of Jordan's memoir, because they summed up the crucible experiences that inspired his lengthy career as an attorney, businessman, civil rights leader, presidential advisor, and agent of positive social change.

"To me, Robert Maddox was not an evil man," Jordan wrote. "He was just an anachronism. And with the brashness of youth, I mentally noted (and counted on) the fact that his time was up. I do not mean just his physical time on earth—but I believed that the 'time' that helped shape him was on its way out. His half-mocking, half-serious comments about my educations were the death rattle of his culture....As far as I was concerned, I was executing a plan for my life and had no time to pause and re-educate him."[10]

Finding my fight was a long process with a key moment coming when I was fired. You might find your fight in a way that doesn't seem as connected to that sort of crucible moment. Maybe you will find it during a retreat that's designed to help you discover your purpose, for instance, or maybe you will simply have an inspired epiphany one morning while sipping coffee and watching the sunrise.

Regardless of when and how you identify your fight, I'm willing to bet you can connect it back to a significant struggle during your journey—something you went through or something you witnessed others going through.

I know my fight is right for me, because my passion for creating a table of prosperity for others compelled me to get up and get back in the game whenever times got tough. The struggle made my fight clearer and more meaningful. Once I found it, however, I couldn't let it fade into the background. I had to move to the next pathway and focus on what really mattered.

---

10   Vernon Jordan Jr., *Vernon Can Read! A Memoir* (New York: PublicAffairs, 2001).

Chapter 4

Pathway 2—Focus on the (Real) Prize

Avoiding distractions keeps you on the right road.

ONE OF THE MOST PIVOTAL moments in my professional career came when I missed out on an opportunity to become president of one of Comcast's divisions.

I had joined the cable industry as a regional vice president for Telecommunications, Inc. (TCI), which later was purchased by AT&T. I soon became the senior vice president of AT&T Broadband's "Atlanta cluster," and I stayed in Georgia as regional senior vice president of the Mid-South after AT&T Broadband merged with Comcast.

The next logical step up would be as president of one of Comcast's divisions, so I worked hard toward that goal. When one of those roles opened, however, I didn't even get a chance to toss my hat into the ring for consideration. Instead, the job went to a former employee who had worked for me at AT&T Broadband. He had joined Comcast as a regional senior vice president about six months prior to the merger, so we were peers when the two companies became one. Now he was moving up, and I was staying put.

It stung to feel passed over, and I battled with giving in to a victim mentality. I had to ask myself what I had done or not done that had cost me the promotion. And I had to fight the temptation to assume race had played a role in the decision-makers' process.

I'm not saying the other guy wasn't qualified—he was extremely qualified. But I had paid my dues and had a stellar track record. I knew in my heart that I was ready for the challenge of running a division. It just didn't *feel* fair, and, frankly, it hurt. Part of me wanted to dust off my résumé and look for a different employer, and part of me wanted to stay angry and lash out at anyone who crossed my path.

Instead, I refocused.

I was enrolled in a program at Harvard at the time, and the professor, also an African American, preached patience.

"You will get there," he said, "just three years later than your white counterparts."

And he was right. Rather than getting distracted by the disappointment, I kept my eye on the real prize and, three years later, I was named president of Comcast's West Division.

MY FRESHMAN LIFE LESSON

Life is full of distractions that keep us from focusing on the things that really matter. That's why my definition of uncompromising includes words like "radically responsible" and "undistracted." If we aren't uncompromising in those areas, we lose focus and put everything we're working for at risk.

The easiest analogy is that it's like driving a car. Failing to master this pathway always sends us on detours from where we need to go and often puts us in a ditch.

I'm sure my mother and other early mentors preached this point when I was growing up, but it really stuck with me because of something a friend told me during my freshman year in college.

Stepping onto the Bloomington campus of Indiana University in the summer of 1978 was in many ways like stepping onto another planet. The fifty-mile trip only took about an hour by car, but I felt like I'd been blasted into outer space.

The town, nestled among hills, forests, and lakes, was home to about fifty thousand people back then, so it was small compared to Indianapolis. The university, however, added another thirty thousand to the mix, so it felt huge to a kid who'd seldom ventured more than a few miles from his inner-city home.

As a first-generation college student, I wasn't sure what to expect when I made the trek into this phase of adulthood. The opportunities, and the temptations, were overwhelming, and I was a typical seventeen-year-old who was eager to step out of the authority of his mother's home and taste all that this big, bright world had to offer. So once I got moved in and began to get acclimated, I started looking into the fraternities.

I'm not sure how it is now, but at Indiana back in those days, fraternities and sororities were particularly important to black students. Imagine showing up as a newcomer to a community with 31,526 people. Many of them know each other already, but you know hardly anyone. You look around at a sea of faces—mostly people who don't look like you or share your background. It's not that you don't want to get to know these people and blend in, but you also long for something familiar.

When I enrolled at IU, in fact, only 4.5 percent of the student body was African American. Fraternities and sororities provided a way for black students to bond based on our shared experiences and to develop a sense of belonging in what, for most of us, was an unfamiliar world.

I thought I'd join one, get plugged into the party scene, and make friends for life. So I mentioned the idea to Stanford Miller, a fellow freshman who also was from Indianapolis. We had attended different high schools, but we had met earlier that summer and quickly become friends. I figured he and I could pick the same fraternity and pledge together.

"Do what you want," he told me, "but I'm not going to do that, and let me tell you why. That's not my purpose for being here. That's not my focus. Anything that will get in the way of my purpose for being here is a distraction, and I'm not going to allow that to happen."

Now, what teenager has that kind of common sense?

For some, the Greek life was just fine, but Stanford—or Lukie, as we called him—was self-aware enough to know it wasn't for him. And I realized it wasn't best for me, either. I was all about the benefits of being in a fraternity, but pledges endured hazing (which often got out of hand in those days) and gave up all their personal freedom to do the bidding of their new "big brothers."

Joining would mean committing to an arduous eight- to ten-week process that would consume my time and energy, and the last thing I needed was to get off to a bad start in college. I needed to carve my own path on campus, and I didn't need the competing demands and priorities that typically come with pledging a fraternity.

Even though I didn't join a fraternity, I did get distracted a time or two from my purpose for attending IU. Or three.

Well, plenty. But I learned that instant gratification is not what it's cut out to be.

The world offers all sorts of prizes, and we can't get distracted by prizes of lesser value.

What are prizes of lesser value? The list is long, but it includes things that feel good in the short term but aren't good for us over the long haul—like getting angry about not getting a promotion. It also includes some good things that aren't aligned with our goals.

The *real* prizes are the ones that add true value in life and help us accomplish our purpose, and those are the ones that require a unique and uncompromising focus.

KEEPING YOUR "UNIQUE" FOCUS

The type of discipline and dedication it takes to stay focused on what matters won't happen on its own, of course. We must be intentional, and we need the help of others to live out this pathway.

In college, I was fortunate to find a band of brothers who helped me focus. Those brothers didn't take the form of a fraternity, but they were something similar. Lukie and I connected with several other guys—Ron "Big Bird" Singletary, Teddy Snowden, Darrius Knuckles, Greg Wright, Bobby Walker, and Thomas Samuel Bailey III ("TSB No. 3")—to form a group we called Unique, Inc.

I'm not sure how we came up with the name, but I know we felt we were different. The normal course was not our course. There was no hazing, no drinking games, no dues, no secret handshakes, and no blood sacrifices. We just made a commitment to navigate college life together.

Unique, Inc., was part social club and part study club. We would throw parties, but we also encouraged each other when life felt exhausting and held each other accountable to staying on track with our education. For instance, we regularly went to the main library on Friday nights and studied among its 4.6 million collection until 8:00 or 9:00 p.m. We put in the work, in other words, before we allowed ourselves to hit the social scene.

The lives of the men who made up Unique, Inc., have played out in very different ways. While some of us found professional and personal success, others struggled. Three of the eight have passed away, including one who was murdered. All of us lost our way at one time or another, but some never really found their way back.

That's why this pathway is so personal to me—it grieves me to think about distractions keeping anyone from reaching their potential or, worse, leading them toward an untimely death.

In my private life and in my professional career, I have often found myself tempted to take my eyes off the prize, but I have found there are several ways we all can be intentional about staying on this important pathway:

Identify your sideshows.

Most of us are self-aware enough to know our weaknesses, even if we might hide them, lie about them, or justify them to others. When no one else is around, however, we can't escape the truth. And the more intentional we are about acknowledging those things that are most likely to distract us, the more effective we are at dealing with them.

Anything that distracts us from accomplishing our goals is a sideshow we should avoid. It takes discipline, but the discipline can't be applied until we've identified our personal sideshows.

When I was in college, I knew parties were a sideshow. If I didn't hit the books on Friday before going out, there was little hope that I would hit them Saturday morning. Or Saturday afternoon. Or Sunday.

John Maxwell, who has written dozens of books related to life and leadership, uses a pearl of wisdom he got from his father to describe how we prioritize our options: "You can pay now, and play later, or you can play now and pay later. But either way, you are going to pay."[11] I knew that putting play first would prove to be a very costly distraction in my life, so I paid on the front end by going to the library before going out.

Another big distraction many of us face comes in how we respond to disappointments, either something of our own making or something that happened that was beyond our control. Earlier I mentioned the importance of avoiding a victim mentality that tends to develop when we've been knocked down. That's because a victim mentality often is a huge distraction that's counterproductive to living a successful life.

When I was fired and when I didn't get the role of president, I was tempted to not only visit the victim sideshow but to take up residency there. Fortunately, with the help of others, I was able to identify the distractions, refocus, and keep moving forward in a positive way.

Have a good chip on your shoulder.

Way back in the early 1800s, a custom apparently evolved among young boys who got into disputes with one another. One boy would put a chip on his shoulder and

---

11   You can find this quote in several of Maxwell's books or articles, including *Today Matters: 12 Daily Practices to Guarantee Tomorrow's Success* (New York: Center Street, 2008).

dare the other to knock it off. I'm not sure what type of chip they used—A potato chip? A poker chip? A cow chip?—but it symbolized a challenge. If the other boy knocked it off, then a fight ensued.

An idiom was born. Now the dictionary defines it this way: "to seem angry all the time because you think you have been treated unfairly or feel you are not as good as other people."[12]

We've all known people with that type of chip on their shoulder. They walk around angry, bitter, and resentful, and they're always looking for a fight because they believe someone—or the world—has done them wrong.

When people do things that aren't fair or say things that aren't kind, it can weigh us down. But it also can lift us up. When my relatives told my mother that her sons would never amount to anything, I heard it and it stuck deep in my subconscious like gum on a shoe. The fact that I still remember it forty-plus years later is an indication of that chip's power. I was determined to prove them wrong. I used it to lift me up.

My chip could have become a distraction to my fight if I hadn't made sure it was a good chip, not a bad chip. In other words, I couldn't let it make me angry, bitter, and resentful. And I couldn't dare people to knock it off or throw my successes in the faces of others with an "I told you so" bravado.

A good chip motivates us to win, but to win the right way and to win the right things. It doesn't lead to fights; it supports our personal fight—in my case, a passion for bringing other people to a table of prosperity. No one

---

12 Cambridge Dictionary, *https://dictionary.cambridge.org/us/dictionary/english/have-a-chip-on-your-shoulder*, last accessed October 2, 2020.

would want to join me at that table if I had a bad chip on my shoulder.

Create an environment that supports your fight.

Once we know our fight and the distractions that tend to take us off track, we can build boundaries and processes that keep us focused.

I do this in several ways. For instance, I try to be the "chief repeater" of my fight. I don't walk down the hallways in our office building mumbling positive reinforcements to myself about creating a table of prosperity for others, but I do regularly restate my fight, often out loud. This can occur in the normal course of conversations with other people, or it might come during my private moments. Consistently repeating the key messages of my life helps create a positive environment in my mind, especially when it seems like the world around me is devolving into chaos.

I also do this by establishing what many leaders call a "kitchen cabinet"—a group of trusted advisors who know what's important to me, know my strengths and weaknesses, and know that they have the freedom to set me straight when I go astray.

Some people, like my wife and Lukie, are permanent members of this group. Others are in my cabinet and don't even know it. And some rotate in or out depending on my season of life or a specific challenge I might be facing. Some might speak more into one aspect of my life— fatherhood or business strategy, for instance—but I do my best to find advisors who are well rounded and can speak to multiple aspects. I want to be a great business leader, husband, father, and man of faith, so I look for advisors who have successfully integrated those roles into their lives.

Another significant part of an environment that supports my fight is developing a shield of armor that protects me against disappointments and other distractions.

Hardly a week goes by when I'm not disappointed in myself over something. It's not always a big something, but the perfectionist in me doesn't even like the little somethings. Other people also let me down from time to time. They show up late, drop the ball at a key point in the game, make bad choices, and generally behave as all humans do—with faults.

A shield of armor helps me stay true to my fight while offering grace and forgiveness to myself and others. It provides the wisdom that comes from a proper perspective on life.

My shield is forged by my daily routines—a devotional and morning prayer, reading over notes that prepare me for my day, listening to podcasts, reading good books and articles, and soaking in or reflecting on the wisdom and encouragement from my kitchen cabinet.

I know challenges will come at me from all directions, and every one of them has the potential to distract me from the *real* prize. Staying focused is not an easy pathway. The question is, how will I respond? And if I've prepared my heart and mind in the right ways, I'm more apt to respond in alignment with my fight.

Suspend your disbelief; open your eyes to the possibilities.

If you ever watched an action movie, you know there are times when you must practice what's known as "suspension of disbelief." The idea, which actually predates movies by several hundred years, is that sometimes an audience willingly ignores the implausible for the sake of enjoying the flick.

Yeah, Dwayne Johnson's character just leaped out of a helicopter onto a moving eighteen-wheeler while dodging machine gun fire on his way to a fistfight with the bad guy. Sure. No problem, at least not for the Rock!

With the movies, we can push pause when it comes to questioning what's truly possible. And the same idea holds true for anyone who wants to live a fulfilling life—the pathway to success involves a fiercely independent belief in your dreams, and the stronger your belief, the more you can stay focused on what really matters.

In life, we can't deceive ourselves by denying reality, but we also need to keep our minds and hearts open to possibilities even when—especially when—others are telling us our expectations are misplaced or that we should give up. If we don't believe in our dreams, after all, no one else will. And if we only believe in the things we can see right in front of us, then we can easily miss out on something greater that's right around the corner.

Perhaps the greatest example I know of someone living out this principle is my wife, Barbita. When we married, we both knew we wanted to start a family. For years, however, we were unable to have a child, even after trying in vitro. The doctors eventually told us we were too old, and it was too risky to keep trying. But she never lost hope and never lost faith that she would someday be a mother.

Every time we moved—eleven times over the years— she would put pink and blue ribbons on the doorknobs throughout the new home as a symbol of her faith. "I'm not going to allow these doctors to get inside my head," she would say. And she would not allow me to give up hope, either. She once added up the time she had spent praying to have a child, and the total was more than five thousand hours.

Then, in 2012, she called with the news: she was pregnant.

At that point, the critics changed their tunes. Now they suggested having a child wasn't a good idea. It was a high-risk pregnancy, but she never allowed those voices to distract her from what mattered—being a mother. Instead, she put herself in a position for a miracle to happen and embraced it when it came along. And today we have a son, Stevie, who, believe it or not, was born on my birthday.

By the way, don't miss the part about how she "put herself in position" to realize her dreams. Barbita prayed for hours, but she also took care of her body, ate right, and made sure that she did everything possible to not only conceive a child but have a healthy pregnancy and delivery. She was focused on what mattered, and she combined her belief with intentional actions.

There are no guarantees in life, of course, and many couples faithfully pray for years to have a child without those prayers being answered in the exact way they wanted. I've come to believe that our part is to worry less about the end results and more about the process, because if we hold true to the process—if we keep our eyes faithfully and obediently on the *real* prize—then the results, even if different from our expectations, ultimately will work out for our good.

You might have a faith that's different from mine and Barbita's, but I believe the principle holds true for everyone. If you want to stay focused on your real prize, you must ignore the implausible and suspend your disbelief.

Stay up even on a down day...or month...or year.

The University of Virginia has experienced many wonderful "firsts" during its two hundred–plus year history, including several that have involved its men's basketball team. In 2018, however, the Cavaliers experienced the type of "first" that no other team would covet. They were the first No. 1 seed in the NCAA Tournament to lose to a No. 16 seed.

The University of Maryland, Baltimore County Retrievers not only pulled off the upset, but they won convincingly—74–54 over a Virginia team that had come in with a 31–2 record.

I wasn't in the locker room after that loss, but I doubt anyone who was there would disagree that it was a down day for the prestigious Virginia program.

When the team came back together after the off-season, head coach Tony Bennett didn't spend the first practice going over the mistakes they had made in the loss or even doing drills to get better. Instead, he put on a video of a TEDx Talk that his wife had shared with him.

The speaker, Donald Davis, told a story about his father, who had been injured in an accident with an ax when he was five years old and soon became known around their small town as Cripple Joe. Rather than embracing that narrative for his life, his grandmother encouraged him to tell the story of his accident every chance he could. When something bad happens to you, she told him, "it sits on top of you like a rock." And the only way to climb out from under that rock and sit on it, she said, is to tell the story.[13]

Cripple Joe told the story over and over. And rather than sinking into depression about his inability to work on the

---

13   Donald Davis, "How the story transforms the teller," TEDxCharlottesville, December 23, 2014, *https://www.youtube.com/watch?v=wgeh4xhSA2Q, last accessed October 8,* 2020.

family farm or unkind nicknames, he climbed from under that rock and he went to business school. He eventually returned to his hometown and became a banker—Banker Joe, as he became known. He had totally rewritten the narrative of his bad day.

"It is never, never tragic when something people think is bad happens to you," Davis said in his talk. "Because if you can learn to use it right, it can buy you a ticket to a place you would never have gone any other way."[14]

The Virginia coaches and players began telling the story about their humbling loss. They told it all season long, they went back to work in the gym, and they got out from under that rock. In fact, after losing in the first round in 2018, the Cavaliers won the national championship in 2019.

Clearly, they weren't defined by their down day.

No one likes bad days. Or bad months. Or bad years. But I've found that giving into anxiety, fear, or depression seldom moves us to a better place. When we face a down day—or a stretch of tough times—I am convinced we can be realistic, serious, and, when the situation calls for it, even somber about the circumstances of life. But we can't allow them to distract us from our real prize.

My response to such troubles begins with an approach that might seem fairly simple: I count my blessings. I realize I don't have all the answers and most things are out of my control. But thinking about the good things in my life—the list is long—helps restore my optimism and my confidence. I remember that I've been down before, and I recall the things that got out from under my personal rocks.

This idea of staying focused on the *real* prize is one of the most challenging pathways of an uncompromising

---

14   Ibid.

life, because life is full of distractions. But if we get knocked off this pathway, we soon find ourselves racing down roads that lead to destruction.

If, on the other hand, we can really develop a fiercely independent, radically responsible, scrappy, and undistracted mindset with an unwavering commitment to our why, then we are ready for the other pathways that will strengthen our fight and produce a life well lived.

Chapter 5

Pathway 3—Live Life as a Learning Lab

Embracing life's lessons keeps you alive and growing.

AMONG MY SMORGASBORD OF FATHER figures growing up was a man affectionately known as Smitty.

Evans Smith worked with Uncle Horace at Citizens Gas and Coke, the gas utility in Indianapolis, and it was through that connection that he met my mother not long after we moved to Indiana.

Smitty had a unique ability to spend time with people and make them feel like they were the most important person in the world to him. He locked eyes, asked questions, and listened with a rapt attention that never came off as anything but heartfelt and genuine.

Smitty was about five foot ten and thick without appearing overweight—a solid, dark-skinned man who looked like he could have been a middle linebacker in his prime. He didn't focus much attention on himself, but you could tell that the unspoken chapters of his life were full of fascinating stories. It was clear his experiences had run the gamut—disappointment, pain, sadness, pride, happiness, joy, and everything in between.

He had served as a noncommissioned officer in the US Army, a sergeant first class who saw action in the Korean War, and he did his blue-collar work for the gas company without complaint. His hair was gone on the top and thin on the sides when we first met, and his hands were hard as bricks. But he had a gentle soul and never dwelled on the injustices of his life or allowed them to steal his joy or strip him of his love for others.

He was easy to like and easier to respect.

Smitty became a frequent visitor to our home, often showing up after work with ice cream for the kids. And, in time, he and my mother became more than just friends. When I went to college, he was right there with Momma to drive me to Bloomington and help me move into my dorm room. A few years later, when I was in my early twenties, he officially became my stepfather. And when he passed away on August 2, 2017, after eighty-nine years of life, Smitty's obituary listed me and my brothers among his children.

From the day he entered my life in the early 1970s until those final hours nearly five decades later, Smitty taught me the value of curiosity and a growth mindset, or what I like to call "living life as a learning lab."

Without an uncompromising commitment to this pathway, I believe we can't really live our best life—because if we aren't learning, we aren't growing, and if we aren't growing, we're just dying.

Smitty modeled the "learning lab" philosophy by never passing up an opportunity to ask questions or seek information that would teach him something new. He was insatiably curious. Every morning, he read at least three newspapers. When he came by the house, he would spend time with us talking about sports and life, sharing nuggets of information and wisdom that guided our paths without us even realizing it. And he was never afraid to try new things, even those that took him out of his comfort zone. I'll never forget the day he told me he was taking Spanish lessons. He was seventy-five!

In 2017, the US government invited Smitty to join other veterans on a trip to South Korea so they could experience the dramatic improvements that resulted in large part from their service decades earlier. Smitty saw it as just another opportunity to learn. On his way back to Indiana, however, he had a heart attack while in the airport in Toronto. Instead of coming "home," he went "Home." But as I was able to share at his funeral, it was a fitting way for him to go—learning and experiencing new things.

For Smitty, to live was to learn. He only had a sixth-grade formal education, but he had a PhD from the school of life. The world around him was a laboratory. And he not only spent time in that lab right up until he took his final breath, but he also helped me make an uncompromising commitment to this pathway. Instead of focusing on the exhaustion of his experience, he modeled what it looks like to never stop growing, never stop living.

THE LIFE OF CURIOSITY

Do you remember the day you were born? Not the date, but the details of the experience?

Me either.

But here's what I know about that day: I arrived curious.

We all do. We show up totally confused by the new environment, and we immediately start trying to figure things out. *What happened? How'd I get here? What's that sound? What's that feeling?* And with each passing hour and each passing day, as our senses come more and more into their own, we go about the lifelong process of learning.

With few exceptions, scientists believe all humans are born curious. And, furthermore, we apparently are the only species that vigorously tries to answer the one-word question, "Why?"

In fact, astrophysicist Mario Livio, author of *Why? What Makes Us Curious*, points out that we all experience "epistemic" curiosity—an innate thirst for knowledge like when we feel compelled to take a toy apart for no other reason than to just see how it works.

"Our brain and our mind assign value to this knowledge," Livio said, "so this is usually experienced as a pleasurable thing, with an anticipation of reward in the form of what we learn."[15]

Epistemic curiosity explains why we intuitively love to learn new things—we are rewarded not only with the actual knowledge but also from the experience of learning it. There's an incredible joy that comes with a new idea or an insight—sitting in a math class when a formula suddenly makes sense, hearing a fresh take on an old idea at a conference, or pulling disconnected information together for a solution to a complex problem at work.

This type of curiosity not only shapes what we know but who we are—our personalities, our worldviews, our passions, and our drive to find and live out our purpose.

---

15   Adam Wernick, "Why are humans so curious?" The World, August 27, 2017, https://www.pri.org/stories/2017-08-27/why-are-humans-so-curious, last accessed June 12, 2020.

One of the first of these light-bulb moments I remember as a kid happened way back in 1969 when our family still lived in Florida. I was visiting my cousins' home one evening, and they were allowed to watch way more television than me and my brothers, so I was pretty excited to gather in the front room with them to watch just about anything.

I looked at the screen that night and saw this young kid about my age with a big Afro and a wide nose on his dark face. He had an electric voice and killer dance moves. And even though he was the youngest member of his group, he commanded the stage in a mesmerizing fashion.

It was one of the first television appearances by Michael Jackson and the Jackson 5, and it woke something up in me that is hard to describe. There was a pride in seeing someone similar to me on television—something extremely rare for black Americans in the 1960s.

I wanted to know more about this singer—how he and his family got on television and what it took to achieve the type of success where people reacted to what you did with thunderous applause and screams of joy.

I was interested in him, of course, but I also was interested in me. *If he can get there*, I thought, *what would it take for me to get there, too?* I never embraced the dream of becoming a famous entertainer, but I became curious about exploring possibilities for my life that I never before realized existed. All I needed to light that spark was exposure to a little bit of oxygen. Michael Jackson was the oxygen, and others in my life would fan that spark into a flame.

I believe an openness to experiencing new wonders is what drives uncompromising people to learn and grow. And when we lack curiosity, it's like throwing water on the candle of our dreams. We don't learn, so we don't grow, so we don't experience what life has to offer.

We never lose our curiosity, scientists say, but clearly it diminishes or goes underdeveloped for far too many of us. As we mature, we settle into routines. We grow more efficient and stick to options that we know will work, that don't take us out of our comfort zones, that don't involve risks to our ego, and that allow us to move quickly in a world that demands speed.

The unfortunate side effect: it often sucks the life out of our childlike wonder. And the more we settle for a less curious mindset, the less information we have at our disposal for problem-solving, the less creative we are in our solutions, the less we feel inspired, and the more we compromise on our real potential in life.

Thankfully, I've found ways to stoke the fires of my curiosity. That's because of all the gifts I was given by people like Smitty, perhaps the best was the endless encouragement to never compromise when it came to exploring the learning laboratory of my life. This gift has taken me to interesting places, taught me useful things, and confirmed the truth in the adage that success is found in the journey, not the destination.

That journey ends when we stop learning new things, because learning is oxygen—it keeps us going, even when it's uncomfortable or painful, and it strengthens us for the challenges and opportunities that come as we pursue our fight.

FROM CURIOSITY TO FIERCE INDEPENDENCE

Asking, listening, and learning at the right time literally set me up for the biggest promotion of my life, but I almost missed it because I initially didn't want to give a new opportunity a chance.

Shortly after I missed out on the opportunity to be president of one of our divisions, I got another job opportunity—senior vice president of the California region. My first reaction? *Thanks, but no thanks.*

Frankly, I was still ticked off because I didn't get the job as president. Not only that, but the new job would require a move to California. We were living in Atlanta at the time. We liked it there, and I had little interest in experiencing the high cost of living in California. Furthermore, I was already a regional senior vice president. I had no desire to pursue what, on the surface, was a lateral career move.

I shot down the idea before it ever took flight.

Call me when I can move up, I thought, *not over.*

One of the counterintuitive qualities of fierce independence, however, is a willingness to listen to trusted advisors when they tell you something you don't really want to hear. And my trusted advisors—especially my wife—all echoed the same response about this job opportunity: *Don't be stupid! Check it out.*

I quickly realized I was letting my wounded pride get in the way of my curiosity, so I took their advice and flew to San Francisco to learn more about the job.

The change in attitude made all the difference. I started asking questions and exploring the options. And I learned there was far more to the opportunity than I had assumed.

I discovered that the president of the West Division was planning to retire in two years. The presidents of our other divisions, meanwhile, all were settled in for the long haul. So this was an opportunity for me to learn the western market and prove myself worthy of what would likely be the next chance for a promotion.

There were no guarantees, and there were others who would compete with me for the job when it opened up, but moving to California would position me to become a prime candidate, provided I performed well, which I did.

Two years later, the president retired and I got the promotion to president of Comcast West, but it never would have happened if I had followed my initial emotional response to close the door on a lateral move without ever asking questions and learning more about it.

Curiosity can't happen unless you are open to it. You have to maintain a fierce independence to break free of peer pressures and herd mentalities so you can explore possibilities when those around you are pulling you toward the status quo. And that takes work—especially when the possibilities don't make much sense, when all you see is the obvious, or when your vision is clouded by the fog of past experiences. You have to stay focused on the prize and independent of the noises that aren't adding value to your fight. Then you can question your assumptions so that curiosity can fill your tank with good information and you can make better decisions about opportunities you otherwise might totally miss.

There are other practical benefits to learning that help us excel as we navigate life. For instance, an emphasis on learning turns mistakes and setbacks into opportunities. By learning from our failures and misfortunes, we're less likely to repeat them and more likely to make better decisions in the future. We're also more willing to take risks, because we know that even failure yields something positive if we're willing to learn from it. There also are health benefits to learning, like reduced stress levels and improved memory.[16]

---

16   John Coleman, "Lifelong Learning Is Good for Your Health, Your Wallet, and Your Social Life," *Harvard Business Review*, February 7, 2017, https://hbr.org/2017/02/lifelong-learning-is-good-for-your-health-your-wallet-and-your-social-life, last accessed July 1, 2020.

A focus on learning also helps us develop humility and empathy, two qualities that are essential to a life that offers grace and builds trust. The more we know, the more we realize how much we still need to learn, and that's humbling—at least it has been for me!

Finally, learning as a lifestyle just feels good. Learning, as Mario Livio noted, is its own reward. It is encouraging, uplifting, and life-giving. The other benefits are icing on the proverbial cake, but of course, the icing is good, too!

All of this comes together as we work toward an uncompromising life, because the commitment to the learning pathway leads to preparation that feeds our self-confidence and allows us to have that all-important fiercely independent mindset. We're humble enough to realize we don't know it all but confident enough in what we do know to lean into it in unwavering but radically responsible ways.

MY REAL-LIFE LAB

I've experienced all those benefits from learning, but never more so than when I accepted a leadership challenge in the summer of 2020. That's when my willingness and ability to live life as a learning lab were put to the test (for reasons some might find a bit surprising) in the weeks and months following the death of George Floyd in Minneapolis.

Floyd was killed on May 25, 2020, when a police officer pinned him to the ground and held his knee on Floyd's throat for nearly ten minutes. As a group of onlookers stood by, including several other officers, Floyd suffocated until he died. Videos of the altercation went viral, and they were shocking and disturbing on countless levels—especially for black Americans who have seen all too many examples of unjustified excessive force and systematic racism in our country.

Barbita and I were watching the news on television the first time we saw the actual video of Floyd's death, and I'll never forget the sinking feelings of sadness, loss, anger, and downright exasperation that overwhelmed me. His story wasn't my story, but it added to the fatigue I felt from the lifetime of my black experience.

I was reminded almost immediately of something I'd heard decades earlier during a diversity training session led by Al Vivian. It was the late 1980s, and I was working for Pepsi when Vivian, the son of famed civil rights leader C. T. Vivian, posed a question to our group: *What have we, as a people, ever done to white people that would promote so much hatred and disharmony?*

Roughly thirty years later, I was asking almost the exact same question: *What have we done as a people that would promote this lack of respect for human dignity?*

I also began contemplating what I should say about all of this to my thirty thousand employees who also were seeing the video and the fallout that came from it. I awoke even earlier than usual the next morning, and it was 3:00 a.m. when I sat in the dim light and silence while writing a six-hundred-word letter that tried to make sense of the senseless. A few days later, after our CEO had sent out a letter of his own, I shared my letter with the employees in the West Division. I told them I was heartbroken over the events for four main reasons.

"First, inclusiveness is critical to our country," I wrote. "Just knowing that a large part of our African American population feels threatened and unsafe is difficult to comprehend. Second, to witness the senseless killing of George Floyd and others is painful. Third, I'm sad for America because we're better than this. Our country was established as a 'beacon of light and hope' for all, and our responsibility as a country is to show others the way. Finally, I have a little seven-year-old African American boy upstairs safely sleeping and anxious to wake up this morning as his summer of fun starts around mid-afternoon. When do I have the 'conversation' with him? How do I protect his innocence while educating him to the realities of life?"

I also told them that I remained optimistic, because I believed in what we, as a company and as a nation, could do to make the future better. And while I truly was optimistic, the news about Floyd had sent me to an emotionally tough place as I reflected on my life, the lives of other African Americans who have had it far worse than me, and the burden I felt as a black leader in corporate America.

I silently wondered if I had done all I could over the years to fight against racism and inequalities as I moved all around the country while climbing the corporate ladder. My fight—to create a table of prosperity where everyone can participate and enjoy life—isn't exclusive to people of color. *Everyone* means *every single one*. But I have felt an undeniable burden that my success should somehow help my entire race.

Have I done everything possible, I asked, *to ensure that my black brothers and sisters had chairs at that table*? And, regrettably, I kept arriving at the same answer: *I could have done more. I could have spoken up more. I could have done more to level the playing fields. I could have mentored more young leaders. I could have done more.*

The thing about an uncompromising mindset is that it holds you accountable to *do* what you say you believe.

That can lead to some tough conversations with the person in the mirror. But it also doesn't allow you to wallow in regrets. So as I processed all that was going on around me in the world, I realized I had to take radical responsibility for learning from my past and do something positive moving forward. Yeah, I had regrets, but I also had new opportunities, and so I made a fresh, unwavering commitment to my fight.

One of the ways I embraced that challenge was by accepting an assignment to chair Comcast's newly created council on diversity, equality, and inclusion. And, to be totally transparent, I knew this role would take me out of my comfort zone and send me deep into the learning lab of life.

As a black man who grew up in the inner city of Indianapolis, you might suspect that I felt like the perfect person to lead this effort. That wasn't the case. I believed I was the *right* person, and I felt a tremendous burden of responsibility to make a positive difference in the role, but I was far from the *perfect* person.

I immediately recognized that for the council to have success, I had to start from the humble reality that I didn't have the answers—in fact, I couldn't even pretend to know all the right questions.

Here was my reality when I agreed to take that assignment: I was a black man with a privileged life. I was not young. I was not poor. I drove a nice car, wore nice clothes, and lived in a nice home with a wonderful wife and a fantastic son who attended one of the best schools in America. I spent more time, professionally and even personally, with white people than with other black people. And I couldn't say I dealt daily or even regularly with overt racism.

I was *sensitive to the struggle*, but I was not *in the struggle*. The edges of this type of injustice and inequality were not as sharp for me as for, say, one of our technicians who works in the field, a retail associate in one of our stores, or a graphic designer in our marketing department. My attitude was not *I'm living this nightmare* or *I've been there and I know*, but rather *I need to ask questions and learn*.

This is where an uncompromising commitment to living life as a learning lab played a practical role in how I led the council. I realized that we needed to come up with our fight on this complex but important challenge. *What would it look like*, I wondered, *for this team to develop a fiercely independent, radically responsible, scrappy, and undistracted mindset around diversity, equality, and inclusion?* To find that answer, and then commit to it in an uncompromising manner, we would have to learn together.

The first thing I did was spend some time alone processing the situation and coming up with a proposed definition for the goal of the council. Then I followed through with a promise I had made in my letter to our employees. I met with every vice president in the West Division, hosted a call with all three thousand supervisors and above, and held a session with ninety-five leaders from our frontline Employee Resource Group. I also met with every black senior vice president in the company. I heard from others who, like me, were sensitive to the struggle, and I talked to several employees who were in the struggle.

After learning as much as I could from those groups, I wrote a five-page document overviewing the objectives and outlining an initial plan of action—not a plan with the solutions, but a plan to find some solutions. It included things like our guiding principles and initial ideas for getting started. I had some things in mind and I knew some things to avoid, but mainly I was creating a road map for learning based on my learning lab experience.

I didn't just need this road map for myself. I needed it to get alignment from the leadership team and from the other people who would join or contribute to the council. We had to start on common ground so we wouldn't look at each other later with confusion about where we were going or how we were getting there. So I started with my thinking but also with a commitment that everyone would be heard.

To get beyond the words, however, we had to bring a diverse group of people together and learn from one another. We had to approach the council as a laboratory, not as a debate stage. If we weren't willing to listen and learn, we would never make much progress. Thankfully, everyone made a genuine effort to understand one another, and, as I'll share in more detail in the next section, that helped us make a positive difference through our work together.

LEARNING IN YOUR LAB

My experience launching the diversity council was a powerful reminder of why this learning lab pathway is so important—because making it a lifestyle prepares us to use a thirst for knowledge and understanding when it matters most. It's not a switch we flip on when needed. It has to be who we are and how we live.

But *how* do we make it a part of who we are and how we live?

I believe the key is to approach everything we do with a goal of learning to understand. Here are four ways I try to do that:

Reflect to understand.

I'm not exactly sure when I became an early riser, but I can tell you that it's been an essential part of my learning lab. Unless I have to catch a flight, I almost never set an alarm. I wake up well before the crack of dawn and get my heart and mind right with intentional reflection.

I've done this for so long that it's become a habit, and I consider it one of the most important ways I prepare for my day. It's easy to go through life on autopilot—to let our routines rule us and drive us into ruts that get us stuck. But when we use them intentionally and intelligently, routines become tools that get us where we need to go. Preparation through daily reflection is one of those routines that provides a powerful opportunity for unleashing curiosity so that learning and growth can take place. That's why I am radically responsible about carving out space to make this reflection happen.

Before I settle in at the desk in my home office and start checking email or working through my to-do list, I mentally pull out a map of my life. I want to make sure I'm on the right highway and that I haven't drifted on some detour.

I ask myself questions about things like where I am, where I need to go, how I'm going to get there, who all will be involved, and how I can serve them. I think about my values and ask myself how well I've lived them in recent days and how I can apply them in the situations I am about to face. I think through the things I don't know but need to learn to make better decisions.

I don't arrive at all the answers—in fact, I typically end up with even more questions!—but I feel ready to attack the day with confidence and purpose.

I am also intentional about my process for recording notes from my reflection and keeping track of my projects. I have a notebook for just about every significant project. I write things down, print things off, and regularly review the notebooks so that I'm constantly learning something new or reinforcing something I've learned.

In addition to my morning routine, I often spend time at a nearby library, sipping coffee while reading without the interruptions that typically come at home or the office. When Comcast asked me to chair the diversity council, for instance, I got a new notebook and scheduled a half day away from the world. I spent my time reflecting on my role, the task force's goals, and all the complex issues that would likely need our attention.

The goal was to move from curiosity to understanding, which would allow me to provide direction and leadership. But that clarity wouldn't come without intentionally reflecting in my learning lab. The result was the five-page document that I used to help launch our work.

Research to understand.

In June 2020, *The New York Times Magazine* published a lengthy opinion piece by Nikole Hannah-Jones that dealt with the controversial issue of reparations. It was titled, "What is Owed," and the subtitle was "If true justice and equality are ever to be achieved in the United States, the country must finally take seriously what it owes black Americans."

I didn't agree with all of the conclusions in the article—I'm not sure reparations are what we need for healing in this country—but I was reminded that the way we develop the fierce independence to be uncompromising is to spend time researching from a variety of sources, including books, articles, podcast, news shows, documentaries, and the like.

This article, for instance, laid out the history of policies and decisions related to the black experience that have led us to where we are. Understanding this history a little better helped strengthen my empathy for those who suffer disproportionately because of unequal systems and overt acts of discrimination. I was reminded, again, for example, that I had it better than many black kids in my neighborhood growing up because I had a mother who used a brief stint on welfare as a hand up rather than a handout, who worked hard, who taught us well, and who pushed us to excellence.

I might not have started life at first base, but I was at least in the batter's box. And because I've achieved some success, my son gets to start out on third base. He's almost home before the game for him even begins. That's not the case for many black Americans, and that's something I can never forget or take for granted.

This pathway requires us to open our minds to information, insights, and experiences that will help us grow into better people so we can have a more positive influence on others.

Once I began working as chair of the council, I sought out articles and books on topics related to our task. I spent much of my summer reading articles from *The New York Times* and *Harvard Business Review*, and our entire council read the best-seller *How to Be an Antiracist* by Ibram X. Kendi. Again, I didn't agree with everything I read,

but I promise you that I learned something from everything I read.

Scan to understand.

The sources from which we can learn are as endless as the
stars in the sky, but we won't learn from any of them if we
don't take a look at what they have to offer. The way I like
to approach this is by scanning the world around me and
mirroring the best of what I see. The idea is to see, learn,
and grow by emulating others.

When I was growing up in Indianapolis, for instance, I
learned from teachers like Ms. Goodrum and Coach Cline,
not just in the classroom or in the gym but anytime I was
around them.

This type of learning continued when I got to Indiana
University. The first class I really remember was an African
American studies course taught by the legendary William
Wiggins. I signed up for that class, frankly, because I
thought it would be an easy A. The course, however, not
only woke me up to black history in a deeply personal way,
but it introduced me to one of the most powerful mentors
I've ever been around.

Dr. Wiggins was a giant of a man—tall and with a thick
beard that made him look like he could just as easily survive with the bears of Alaska as with the sharks of aca-
demia. I sat in the front of his class and raised my hand
at every opportunity, as was my practice, and soon I was
among the students who would get regular invitations to
his home for dinner.

Two things stand out from what I learned from
Dr. Wiggins.

First, his lectures and the books he recommended
taught me about the unique role blacks played in the his-

tory of America. I understood how proud I should be of the men and women who had fought in wars, made important discoveries, created life-changing inventions, and contributed to every area of culture and society.

Second, his dinners taught me life by example. These weren't dine-and-dash types of meals. You didn't pop in, grab a few bites, and hit the road. No, sir! You showed up and socialized. Then you sat down at the table with him, his family, and the other guests for a feast that typically lasted at least ninety minutes. It didn't take nearly that long to eat, of course, but the main serving at these meals was the discussions.

I learned a lot from those conversations, but the main takeaways were from what I observed about how Dr. Wiggins lived his life. He modeled a life worth mirroring. It was clear by his actions, for instance, how much he loved his wife, Janice, and their young daughter. He was gentle and loving with them both, and to this day, I hope that I can reflect what I learned from him as a husband and father.

By paying attention with a curious mindset, I learned from what I scanned. Then I mirrored it by putting my new understandings into practice and, more importantly, by paying them forward to others.

Connect to understand.

Not long after the George Floyd incident, one of my colleagues shared a dilemma within her family. Her father had been a policeman for more than thirty years in a major metropolitan area with no known blemishes on his record. But because the reputation of law enforcement officers has been sullied by the high-profile actions of the bad apples, my colleague's teenage daughter decided all cops were awful. Therefore, she wanted nothing to do with her grandfather.

What was missing in their relationship, and what's often missing in relationships where there is intense conflict, is the art of listening, which, of course, begins with a willingness to connect with others in a personal way. The grandfather and granddaughter would have benefited greatly from sharing a table and listening to each other with a heart for learning and understanding.

It's easy to live in an echo chamber rather than a learning lab. In the echo chamber, all you hear is other people who echo what you already believe. In a learning lab, you hear from people who offer a different perspective. Sometimes it's a better perspective, and sometimes it's not. But you never know unless you listen.

This is why the diversity council invited contributors of all races, all levels of employees, and all types of beliefs and backgrounds. We needed all sorts of differences, just as long as we had at least one thing in common: a willingness to listen to each other with the goal of understanding.

Because we had that, we developed solutions that made a difference. In the first few months after we organized the council, for instance, we held a two-hour training on unconscious bias for every employee in the company. We shut the entire company down so everyone could attend, which drove home the importance of the topic.

We also launched the Comcast Rise program, a commitment to helping people of color in small and medium-size businesses by providing them equipment, internet access, commercial production, free ads, and marketing advice, as well as grants of up to $10,000. And we started a new channel on our Xfinity network that airs nothing but stories that highlight successful, non-stereotypical examples of black people.

By creating a learning lab that listened up, down, and all around, we created an even larger learning lab of education and learning throughout our company and with our customers.

The thing about connecting in this way, though, is that it's not easy. We sometimes hear things we don't like or don't agree with. But when we listen respectfully to others, we demonstrate that we value their ideas. And in my experience, connecting to others—listening to them with the goal of understanding—makes them more willing to listen to what we have to offer as well. Then we can learn together.

We could lock ourselves up in a library, read books for hours, and never interact with anyone. We would learn a great deal of information, but to what end? Sure, there would be some joy in the learning, but that joy multiplies by sharing it with others, using it to the benefit of others, and learning from what they can teach us. The learning lab of life is an investment in You, Inc.—and that's the next pathway. But like all investments in You, Inc., it's meant to be experienced with others.

Chapter 6

Pathway 4—Think and Act Like a Business

Investing in You, Inc.

A COMMON THREAD RUNS THROUGH the tapestry of every major change I've ever made in my career: I was thinking and acting like a business.

That includes countless new assignments, dozens of different job titles, and fourteen moves from one city to another. But no change represents this pathway more fully than the one that happened late in 2020 when I stepped down as president of Comcast West and began devoting my time in three primary areas—family, philanthropy, and business.

In addition to spending more time with Barbita and Stevie (family), this move allowed me to give more energy to teaching, speaking, coaching, and writing (philanthropy) while still working part-time as a board member for four publicly traded companies and as special counsel to the CEO of Comcast Cable (business).

When we announced this change, we shared the details about when I was leaving, who was taking my place as president, what I would be doing going forward, and how we would make the transition. Several people approached me later and said something like, "I can't believe how planned out this all is." For me, it was the natural result of thinking and acting like a business.

I see myself as the leader of Me, Inc.—or, as I prefer, SAW, Inc. (Steven A. White). I am the chairman and CEO. As Jay-Z famously put it, "I'm not a businessman, I'm a business, man." Barbita, meanwhile, is chairwoman and CEO of Barbita, Inc. And at the same time, our family is really one unified company, and we are equal partners in our business.

You are the leader of You, Inc., and your success—however you define it—depends on how well you invest in yourself by thinking and acting like a business.

This pathway isn't particularly complicated, and most of us follow it instinctively when we are aware of the need. The challenge is to make it a lifestyle and not just an event we do only during those times when it's an obvious choice.

As any business leader will tell you, however, consistently traveling this pathway isn't easy. We make mistakes. Our emotions distract us. There are competitive forces working against us. And the market is always changing, often in ways that we can't predict or control. But when thinking like a business becomes something we do as naturally as breathing, it guides our actions. Our personal businesses thrive, and others want to invest in us and have us invest in them.

Thinking and acting like a business—in all parts of my life, not just in my career—shapes every decision I make, small and large. It challenges me to separate emotions from facts so that I can act intentionally in ways that align with my values, move me toward my why of creating a table of prosperity for others, and reap the fruits of a more meaningful life.

THE TRANSITIONING OF SAW, INC.

When I consider how a good business "thinks," several characteristics come to mind. Businesses, for instance, are mission-focused and value-driven. They also are objective, unemotional, and pragmatic. They value proven processes. And they are innovative.

All those things were part of my mindset as I made decisions that led me into my newest phase of life.

By 2017, after spending nearly forty years in the corporate world, I was feeling mentally, physically, and emotionally drained. I realized I didn't have the same energy that once came more easily, nor did I still feel the same tension—the butterflies in my stomach each Sunday evening as I prepared for the challenges of another week. I thrived on that tension. It built new muscles in me the same way the tension of lifting weights builds new muscles in the body.

Businesses that are successful for the long haul recognize when something is amiss, and they have an innovative mindset that helps them create a new future. They see change in the wind and allow it to fill their sails. I knew change was in the winds of my sails, and it was time to reinvent how I went about life.

As I stepped back and looked at my situation as a business, I knew that any decisions I made needed to be mission-focused and value-driven. The best businesses know exactly why they exist. Then they prioritize their strategies and plans to support that fight. They create a long-term vision, short-term goals, guiding principles, and supporting strategies and tactics. Everything they do aligns with their mission. So it was essential that my next move align with my mission of creating a table of prosperity for others.

The mission of any good business also revolves around creating value in the marketplace. Their fight is found at least in part by answering a single question: *What can we do or provide that customers will want badly enough to pay us for doing it or providing it?* Every solid business plan includes a clearly articulated value proposition. This gets the attention of investors and draws clients and customers by demonstrating that the business has a legitimate reason to exist. So my next move not only needed to align with my personal values, but it also had to add value to the lives of those around me.

I soon concluded that it was time to retire from one role and come up with new ways of living out my why, but business leaders don't make major decisions in a vacuum. I'll never forget telling my wife about my idea, because it led to a series of significant conversations. I had thought it through and was ready to go. She had several legitimate concerns, including whether we were ready financially for that type of change.

What does a business do when one leader has a big idea and other leaders aren't on board? The leadership team works through it together. They listen to each other. They take in the other person's perspective. They separate their emotions from the discussion and make a pragmatic assessment of what's best for the business. When I finally got my emotions out of the way, I was able to ask Barbita what needed to happen for her to feel comfortable with this change. Then we adjusted my plan to become our plan.

Emotions are a powerful force, and they serve an important role in our decision-making, so I'm not suggesting that you never consider how you or others "feel" about a decision. Seldom, however, do you find a business that consciously makes decisions that it knows will lead to bankruptcy. And businesses that are consistently ruled by emotions tend to make poor decisions that can cost them their mission.

Amy Morin, author of 13 *Things Mentally Strong People Don't Do*, pointed out in an article for *Psychology Today* that good decisions result from a balance of emotions and logic. When we get out of balance, she said, several things can happen that lessen our chances for success. Excitement can cause us to overestimate our chances of success. Anxiety in one area of life can spill over into other areas. Feeling sad can cause us to set lower goals. And anger and embarrassment can result in rash decisions with high-risk, low-payoff choices.[17]

Thinking with the right balance of emotions and logic allows us to make tough decisions in a fair way and still act on those decisions in ways that honors human dignity.

Barbita and I eventually agreed that I would set a goal of leaving the presidency role by the end of 2019, and that goal shifted to 2020 in part because it gave me more time to prepare the table of prosperity for my successor.

As I formalized my goals for the next phase of my life, I began working through an intentional process that sorted through the details. For instance, I consulted some trusted advisors who helped me give definition to the next phase of my life. I also worked with the leadership team at Comcast on an exit strategy that would best serve them

---

17 Amy Morin, "4 Ways Emotions Can Screw Up Your Decisions," *Psychology Today*, February 21, 2016, https://www.psychologytoday.com/us/blog/what-mentally-strong-people-dont-do/201602/4-ways-emotions-can-screw-your-decisions, last accessed June 29, 2020.

and me, which led to the innovative new role we created for my ongoing work with the company.

I approached the move, in other words, very much in the same way that Comcast approached it. The leadership team considered the mission of Comcast and how I could continue to add value to the company. They were objective, unemotional, and pragmatic. And that line of thinking led us to an innovative investment. I am investing in Comcast, and Comcast is investing in me, because we both were thinking and acting like a business.

INVESTING IN YOU, INC.

My responsibilities in life don't end with me, but they begin with me, so a successful life must include an unwavering investment in SAW, Inc. And your success is tightly linked to your investment in You, Inc.

Is that selfish? It depends on the type of business you want to build. If you are a self-absorbed narcissist, then you no doubt will build a selfish "company" that takes more than it gives. You'll get assistance only if you can force it from a position of power, and you'll find respect more elusive than a bipartisan compromise in Washington, DC.

If, on the other hand, you want a "company" that has a positive impact on your partners and the community around you, then that's the type of You, Inc., that you should build. But to achieve your personal goals, including a goal of serving others, you must invest in yourself in much the same way businesses invests in themselves.

This is the approach I've tried to take for most of my life, and it's the approach I've seen in the career of NFL quarterback Tom Brady, including when he made the decision to become a snowbird and fly south to Florida. Brady invested in the New England Patriots for twenty years by investing in himself. Then he invested in himself by going to the Tampa Bay Buccaneers, where he began investing in that franchise.

Brady knows his why. His lifestyle and mindset reflect a daily investment in the things that help him achieve what's important to his You, Inc. He has a long history of taking care of his body with a healthy diet and exercise, but also of spending hours studying film so that he knows more about his opponents than they know about themselves. And he consistently gives his best during hours and hours of practice with his teammates. Why? He wants to give Tom Brady, Inc., the best opportunity to win.

That doesn't mean he lets greed drive his decisions. There were years when he invested in his personal goals by restructuring his contract in ways that helped New England afford to pay more to other players who could help the team succeed on the field. He decided it was in his best interest to take less money if it meant the team might win more games. And in 2020, he invested in himself by accepting an offer to play for Tampa Bay, where the weather was warmer, his financial rewards were sweeter, and he had fresh motivation to win outside of the Patriots' long shadow.

In my view, Brady's departure from New England said as much about his business plan for himself as it did about the business plan of the Patriots, who let him go because they felt it was in the best interests of the franchise.

That type of investing in You, Inc., takes intentional, uncompromising effort. It isn't easy to think and act like a business—to make it part of who you are—but I believe you can do it if you are disciplined about investing in the right mindset in a few critical ways.

Be an owner, not a renter.

Ralph Roberts owned a profitable business in Philadelphia and had every reason to believe the future would be even better than the past. Then, in 1961, he saw a newspaper advertisement for beltless slacks. In a flash, Roberts knew it was time for a change.

Roberts, you see, was president of the Pioneer Suspender Company, which manufactured men's belts, wallets, and jewelry like cuff links and tie bars. He realized a huge chunk of his business was about to fall victim to the whims of style, so in a move some thought was a bit crazy, Roberts sold the company to a competitor.

Two years later, he did something that seemed even crazier: he bought a tiny cable system based in Tupelo, Mississippi, that had a grand total of 1,200 subscribers. Maybe you've heard of it. Now it's known as Comcast, and it's a $105 billion media and technology company.

One of the things I admired most about Ralph was that he always took a long-term view of the business. And the same is true of his son, Brian, who has been CEO of the company since 2002 and overseen much of its most dynamic growth. Like his father, Brian is building Comcast as an owner, not a renter.

Renters take a different view of their surroundings because they seldom plan to stay around for long. Maybe they'll spruce up the walls with some fresh paint, and maybe they won't. Maybe they'll plant some flowers and a few trees, but then again, maybe not. Maybe they'll fix that hole they knocked in the wall, or maybe they'll leave it for the next tenant.

Anyone who has ever owned rental property knows that one of the most important line items in the budget is "maintenance and repairs," especially when a tenant moves out. And renters aren't going to invest in the long-term value of the property. If the countertops and appliances need replacing or the place needs a new roof, that's up to the owner.

Responsible owners know there might be a day when they will sell their company (as Ralph Roberts did with Pioneer Suspender Company) or pass it on to another generation (as he did with Comcast). Until that day comes, however, they are careful to nurture what they own and build it into the best it can be. They spend money on routine maintenance to avoid larger repairs in the future, and they look for ways to continuously improve and sometimes to reinvent themselves.

The Roberts family has consistently made a long-term investment in the success of Comcast, and that's a big reason for the company's success. When we are investing in ourselves, we also should take a long-term view of our lives and our impact. We need to plant trees for the future, regardless of whether we will stick around long enough to enjoy the fruit or the shade.

Don't make it personal.

An uncompromising approach to life involves radical responsibility, not just easy responsibility. Radical responsibility means we do the hard, right thing, which often means setting aside our wounded pride so we can make the best choices for our lives.

I'll never forget how Brian Roberts lived this out in 2014 when a proposed acquisition of Time Warner Cable fell through.

The $45.2 billion deal would have had a huge impact on the industry, and, of course, it drew more than its fair share of opposition. Groups that felt it would have given Comcast too much influence over the broadband market made their case in the court of public opinion as well as with the Federal Communications Commission and the Department of Justice. And after fourteen months of effort, Brian abandoned the idea.

"I really am OK and looking forward to what comes next for our company," he told CNBC. "It is an exciting time in the media landscape."[18]

After the deal officially died, Brian got a phone call from the CEO of one of the nation's largest video content providers, a man who had been adamantly and vocally opposed to a Comcast–Time Warner union. I don't know if he gloated about his victory, but I do know that the conversation included something you might find surprising: they talked about a deal for ensuring that his streaming service was included with all of Comcast's packages. Six months later, they had reached an agreement.

Because he didn't make the opposition or the outcome personal when the Time Warner deal derailed, Brian was able to be radically responsible and move forward with another deal that was good for Comcast. He easily could have held a grudge, but his responsibility wasn't to his ego, it was to Comcast. He was humble enough to accept the fact that things didn't turn out the way he had hoped, and he didn't let the previous disagreements get in the way of a deal that was in the best interest of his customers, his company, and its shareholders.

18   Roger Yu and Mike Snider, "How Comcast, Time Warner Cable deal unraveled," USA Today, April 24, 2015, https://www.usatoday.com/story/money/2015/04/24/how-comcast-deal-to-buy-time-warner-cable-fell-apart/26313471/, last accessed July 10, 2020.

Many of us make our conflicts personal, and it damages the value of our personal You, Inc. We hold grudges. We live in unforgiveness. We don't speak to people we once claimed to love, much less join them for Thanksgiving dinner, because they said something or did something that offended us. Instead, we allow bitterness and envy to rule our emotions, and we miss out on all the joy the relationship has to offer. Even if a relationship isn't salvageable, we only hurt ourselves when the pain someone caused us dictates how we experience life.

Let me put it this way: If someone hurts you and abuses you, do you want that person to be CEO of You, Inc.? Certainly not! You might keep them around or you might never speak to them again, but you don't allow them to sit in your chair and run your life. When you are bitter and unforgiving, however, that's exactly what happens. You step out of your C-suite office and your pain gets to call the shots.

Don't go it alone.

The gig economy has given rise to a new type of worker known as "solopreneurs." These typically are experts in a specific area who contract out their work to businesses that need it. They have no partners and no employees.

Still, they don't succeed on their own. They need mentors and peer advisors, and they need other experts who can complement their work. They need people.

We weren't made to do life alone. Businesses know this, which is why the modern economy puts such a premium on talent. Every business wants to hire the best workforce possible because it gives them a competitive advantage. And the best businesses also turn around and invest in that workforce.

So one way to invest in You, Inc., is by surrounding your-self with people who share your values and will support your vision for the future. They believe in you. And they believe in your fight.

If you are a CEO running a billion-dollar company, you want to surround yourself with smart leaders you can trust who will make deposits in your leadership and help the company succeed. If you are a single mother with three boys, you want to surround yourself with friends and fam-ily you can trust who will make deposits into your life so that you can win as a parent.

At the same time, you have to make deposits into the lives of the people around you.

The importance of taking care of the people who get you where you are going is a lesson I learned in 1997 when I was still a younger leader working for a different cable company. I went along with a corporate plan for cut-ting expenses by freezing the salaries of our most senior employees, regardless of their level in the company. The problem with the plan was that we had a great many long-time employees who took home relatively small paychecks. They had started in low-paying jobs, sometimes minimum wage, and worked their way up, but a salary freeze would be disproportionately difficult for them to handle.

An older technician who worked for me set me straight.

"Steve," he said, "you have two responsibilities: respect your employees and make sure my W-2 goes up every year."

I had failed to fight for his prosperity, so why would I expect him to fight for mine?

Investing in You, Inc., doesn't mean that you don't invest in others. In fact, sometimes the best investment you can make in your future is to invest time, energy, and money in the people around you. I invest in my wife and my friends, for instance, at every opportunity. I want to see them succeed, regardless of my own success. But their success almost always makes my life better, too.

EARNING IT

I learned early in life that when you take full ownership of You, Inc., you won't allow yourself to be a victim. Instead, you take radical responsibility as the owner for whatever circumstances you are in and whatever results you are getting. Everything might not be your fault, but it's still up to you to make it better.

I adopted this mindset at least in part because victimhood just seemed like such an unfruitful path. I saw so many people when I was growing up who seemed stuck in their anger and bitterness, unable to enjoy life, because they felt life had treated them so unfairly.

I wasn't sure if I could overcome the challenges that were part of my life growing up, but I knew this: I wasn't going to surrender to a victim mentality.

Businesses don't think like a victim. They don't enter relationships thinking that customers or clients owe them their business. They know they must earn that business. They have to offer better pricing, better customer service, better hours, better products, and better services—not just once, but every time.

Sometimes they do everything right and the customer still picks a competitor. Sometimes the competitor lies, cheats, or steals to get a piece of a business. The world is harsh, competitive, and often unfair, but businesses can't dwell on those realities. Instead, they look for solutions and opportunities to develop into something amazing, and they go to work trying to make it happen.

I've never allowed myself to believe anyone owes me a thing in life. I got here from different circumstances than most executives, but no one owed me anything. I had to go earn it—the raise, the promotion, the leadership of an important project or piece of business, a voice at the table with other top decision-makers. Sometimes I didn't get what I had earned, so I went to work finding a new or different way to prove I deserved them. That's the bootstrap mindset that has guided me and many other successful people.

You have no bootstraps, you say? Come on! If you are breathing, you have something to offer.

Aimee Mullins had no legs below her knees—literally no place to put boots, much less bootstraps. She learned to walk using prosthetic legs. Then she learned to run—so well that she competed for Georgetown University's track team. Then she set three world records at the 1996 Paralympic Games. After that, she strapped six-inch heels on her prosthetics, walked down the runway as a model for famed designer Alexander McQueen, and went on to become the face of a L'Oréal makeup advertising campaign.

"It's factual to say I am a bilateral-below-the-knee amputee," Mullins said in an interview with ABC News. "I think it's subjective opinion as to whether or not I am disabled because of that. That's just me."[19]

Everyone experiences unfairness, oppression, and injustice, and some people get far more than their share of it.

19 Matthew Rosenbaum and Lana Zak, "Aimee Mullins: Double Amputee a Model, Athlete, Inspiration," ABC News, November 30, 2012, https://abcnews. go.com/US/aimee-mullins-double-amputee-model-athlete-inspiration/ story?id=17851813, last accessed July 13, 2020.

I experienced more of it than many executives I know but not nearly as much as many other people have endured. And we all know the playing field isn't always level.

Society has a responsibility to fix the playing field. In the meantime, and even after that field gets leveled, we have our individual responsibility to work as hard and smart as possible in pursuit of a better life for ourselves.

Thinking like a business on behalf of You, Inc., won't guarantee success, but it will ensure that you stay on the pathway toward achieving your fight. It ensures that you won't give in to a victim mentality. That you won't end life with regrets about what you *didn't get* or how the world never paid you what it owed you. That you won't take success for granted or see failure as inevitable. And that you will do your part to maintain a mindset that feeds your attitude and effort—the only things you can really control, and the key components of the next pathway. That's how you think like a business. That's how you invest in You, Inc.

Chapter 7

Pathway 5—Own Your Attitude and Your Effort

You can only control what you can control.

MY FIRST YEAR AS PRESIDENT of Comcast West could not have gone much better. We relocated from California to Colorado in 2010, found a nice home in a great neighborhood, and I made a smooth transition into the new role. The team around me was great, and we met or exceeded all our goals.

The next year, however, things began to change, and not for the better.

I'll never forget our monthly conference call that April with our CEO. My team was there as I weakly explained why we were missing our numbers—not just by a little, but by a wide margin. It was painful for all of us because there were no extenuating circumstances. We couldn't blame the weather, the competition, the government, a pandemic, or anything else. There was no fragrance I could spritz on our story to make it smell better. There was only this reality: we had failed to get the job done.

When I looked at my team that day, I saw something in their faces that no leader wants to see—they were losing confidence in me. Mentally and emotionally, they were on the verge of checking out. And if I lost them, I knew I might never get them back.

How I responded in the days and weeks to come would determine whether we continued toward a dumpster fire of a year, and I felt the pressure of the situation.

I didn't want to get it wrong for lots of reasons. For one, I felt the pressure to represent my race as the rare black leader to hold this high of an office. I knew other black leaders looked up to me, and I didn't want to let them down. I also suspected there were people who saw me as a token black leader who eventually wouldn't be able to handle a spot at the top of the totem pole. I didn't want to prove them right. But I also felt the pressure to live up to my own expectations. I had finally achieved one of my most long-sought career goals, and I expected success.

So what would I do? How would I respond?

This wasn't the first time I had hit a rocky patch in my leadership journey, and it wouldn't be the last. As with those other times, I could trace the problem to a common cause: I had strayed from my uncompromising approach. In this case, I had stopped trusting myself to lead the way I knew in my gut was best. Rather than leading in a style that worked for me, I had been leading the way I thought others expected me to lead.

A corporate president typically plays the role of a coach, giving other leaders plenty of room to run their business segments and staying out of the details. So that's what I had done. My style had always been to be part of the process, and that's what was missing in 2011. I knew I had to be more involved in developing plans and solving problems—not micromanaging, but trusting my gut to add value when and where I was needed.

Additionally, I had pushed the organization too hard and with too many initiatives, and as a result, we weren't focused enough on any of them. Not only that, but I was so removed from the details that I didn't see the troubled waters until we were neck-deep in them.

The temptation in these situations is to take control. I've seen many leaders do this. They take over—everything. They make every decision. They force their opinions. They make it all about themselves. They try to control the strategy, the tactics, the competition, the markets, the weather...everything. It seldom ends well.

My response was to refocus on what only I could control, and that really boiled down to just two things—my attitude and my effort.

Rather than blaming others and trying to change things that were out of my control, I went back to work with an uncompromising mindset about staying true to myself and working as hard as I could with a positive attitude about our ability to turn things around. I still had to make decisions about things like changes to our strategy and how we would prioritize our efforts, but I couldn't control the past, I couldn't control whether new decisions would work out as planned, and I couldn't control the people around me.

By owning my attitude and my effort, however, I could have no regrets about whatever would happen next. An uncompromising commitment to this pathway means we don't have to second-guess, because we know we did all we could do.

Thankfully, my team fed off my renewed energy and passion. When I showed them that I believed, they started to believe as well. Results came later and that fed confidence, but it started with me having a positive attitude about myself, about my team, and about our path to success. Then we all backed a positive attitude with hard work.

We focused on fewer key priorities, eliminated distractions, and changed the narrative. That October, we presented our 2012 budget plan with great confidence, and the results also began to show up in how we hit our numbers.

Comcast has "power rankings" for all of its divisions that are based on a variety of metrics in areas like operations and customer experience. And because solid performance followed attitude and hard work, the West Division got back to number one in the company's power rankings—and stayed there month after month and year after year. But it started with me owning my attitude and effort, the only things I could truly control when it felt like we were spiraling into chaos.

OWNING YOUR RESPONSE

Condoleezza Rice was the keynote speaker at a conference I attended a few years ago, and I'll never forget a story the former secretary of state told that speaks to the value of owning your response.

Rice spent her formative years in Alabama during the 1950s and early 1960s, and those were turbulent times for America. Leaders like Martin Luther King Jr. had launched the civil rights movement, and Birmingham, where Rice was born in 1954, was an epicenter of the segregated South that saw more than its share of race-related confrontations. Most notably, the Birmingham Campaign, a series of peaceful lunch counter sit-ins, boycotts of businesses, and protest marches that began in 1963, were met with high-pressure fire hoses and snarling police dogs.

The images of violence against African Americans during those years helped sway public opinion nationally and usher in important reforms, but they also told visual stories of the price of change. And Rice's family, like many others, had to make daily decisions about the actions they would take to help create a better world.

Rice's father, John Wesley Rice, was a high school guidance counselor and a Presbyterian minister. Her mother, Angelena, was a schoolteacher. They supported the goals of the civil rights movement but didn't march in protests in part because they didn't want to put their daughter in harm's way.

Both were second-generation college graduates who had used education as a cornerstone to build a middle-class life for their family, and they worked hard to give Rice every opportunity for an even better future. That started with the gift of confidence that comes with education and preparation. She began taking piano lessons when she was three or four, was reading fluently by age five, took dance lessons, learned to play the flute, and would become fluent in French.[20]

While her parents were observers more than participants in protests, Rice said during the conference I attended that her mother and father also taught her to stand her ground. Instead of telling his only child to go along to get along, Rice said her father gave her a different

---

20 Dale Russakoff, "Lessons of Might and Right," *The Washington Post,* September 9, 2001, https://www.washingtonpost.com/archive/lifestyle/magazine/2001/09/09/lessons-of-might-and-right/e3c9f9e2-5f42-420e-b86f-d33abbc7bf42/, last accessed July 15, 2020.

message: *If someone doesn't want to sit by you, you make them move, not you.*

Rice's parents recognized that their daughter couldn't control what other people thought of her, what other people believed, or how other people behaved. She could, however, control her response.

This was a lesson she learned well and applied often. As a freshman in college, for instance, she stood up from among more than two hundred students in a lecture class and challenged a professor who was promoting a theory about white genetic superiority when it came to intelligence. While she recognized she couldn't control this professor or his beliefs, her hard work and attitude had prepared her to respond in an informed, mature, and emotionally intelligent way.

In our pursuit of the best possible life, one thing we can count on is that control is mostly an illusion. We might think we're going to go to this college or get that job or move to a particular city or marry a certain person, but in the end, we have no guarantees that we can make such things happen.

The fallout from the 2020 coronavirus pandemic exemplified this reality. People who were sure about things like travel plans, businesses strategies, and social engagements on one day found themselves "sheltering in place" the next day.

The idea of surrendering control, however, is a challenge for many high-achieving goal setters. We're driven by a book full of aphorisms: *Plan the work and work the plan.... If you can believe it, you can achieve it.... Follow your dreams (or your gut, or your heart).*

It's not that there is no wisdom in those clichés; I am a big-time planner, goal setter, and dream/gut/heart follower.

The problem comes when we try to control those things that are outside of our control—things like the actions of other people or the results of our good intentions.

Maybe you've heard sportscasters talk about teams that "control their destiny." That's nonsense, of course, because destiny, by definition, is something that will happen no matter what. It can't be controlled. But while we can't control our destiny, we can actively take part in it by exercising our free will and doing the next right thing.

Ultimately, I've found that the best way to control our responses to the challenges and opportunities that come our way is to be fiercely independent, radically responsible, scrappy, and undistracted in our commitment to the right attitude and our best effort. Otherwise, we're settling for something less than our best.

This isn't a step in a process, by the way; it is an essential element to all the pathways discussed in this book. In other words, the concept of controlling only what we can control will help us find our fight, focus on the real prize, live life as a learning lab, invest in You, Inc., navigate uncertainty, and commit to road-dog relationships. And all those things support our commitment to owning our attitude and effort. They all work together, sort of like a mosaic of differently shaped pieces that form art when put together properly.

ATTITUDE: THINKING MAKES IT SO

The piece I would put in the center of that mosaic is owning your attitude. In fact, if I were to point to one thing that has most helped me deal with the exhaustion of my black experience, it would be my commitment to owning my attitude.

My wife's grandfather loved to quote William Shakespeare on this topic: "There is nothing either good or bad, but thinking makes it so." (*Hamlet*) How we think about the world around us becomes our reality. And while my reality is shaped by my exhaustion, that exhaustion won't define me—not so long as I own my attitude.

For example, Barbita and I often find ourselves in social and business situations where we are the only black people in the room. We don't exactly blend in, and other people who don't know us sometimes give us a curious look that tells us they are surprised to see us in that environment.

Because we know we belong, our response is to kill them with kindness. That's our attitude. Life is too short to stay angry or bitter over things we can't control, so we choose to own an attitude of loving others as we'd liked to be loved. Part of that, for me at least, is recognizing that's it's not my role to judge others, especially for things I'm sometimes guilty of doing myself.

We've all found ourselves in situations where we were tempted to let the environment or other people have an undue influence over our attitude. We want confirmation that we belong, that we're accepted, that we measure up. When those things are absent, we can be quick to blame others or doubt our self-worth. And when we surrender our attitude to outsiders, we put our success, and at times our very survival, at risk.

I doubt anyone has ever made this point about the importance of controlling our attitude more powerfully than Viktor Frankl. He called attitude the "last of the human freedoms" in his classic book, *Man's Search for Meaning*. We are all free, in other words, to choose our attitude, regardless of the bondage the world might imprison us in.

This was more than theory for Frankl. It was by adopting an attitude that his life had meaning and purpose that he survived the physical, mental, and emotional tortures of Nazi concentration camps during the Holocaust.

This isn't a one-time decision but a daily recommitment. Theologian Henri Nouwen spoke to this when he said, "Joy does not simply happen to us. We have to choose joy and keep choosing it every day!"[21]

More and more, science backs the idea that we benefit from a positive attitude. Research released in 2013, for instance, found people with a family history of heart disease are one-third less likely to have a cardiovascular event like a heart attack if they have a positive rather than negative outlook.[22] Whether it's reducing anxiety, helping you learn, improving your sex life, or upping your game on the basketball court, attitude matters.

EFFORT: MAKE THINGS HAPPEN

Effort, of course, also matters. A great attitude motivates you, but you still have to act. The more effort you put into your actions, the better your odds of success. On the other hand, if you don't put forth effort—or put forth very little effort—you can pretty well count on failure as a result.

As the old saying goes, "Some people watch things happen. Some people make things happen. Some people wonder what happened."

21 Henri J. M. Nouwen, *Here and Now: Living in the Spirit* (New York: Crossroad, 1994).
22 Lisa R. Yanek, Brian G. Kral, Taryn F. Moy, Dhananjay Vaidya, Mariana Lazo, Lewis C. Becker, and Diane M. Becker, "Effect of Positive Well-Being on Incidence of Symptomatic Coronary Artery Disease," *American Journal of Cardiology* 113, no. 8 (October 15, 2013), https://www.ajconline.org/article/S0002-9149(13)01280-0/fulltext, last accessed July 15, 2020.

Actually, there are lots of great aphorisms about the value of taking action. There's an English proverb, for instance, that says, "A man of words, and not of deeds, is like a garden full of weeds." And a Persian proverb that says, "Thinking well is wise; planning well wiser; doing well wisest and best of all." But I really like this one of unknown origins: "No bees, no honey. No work, no money."

My point, however, isn't so much that hard work is important—we all know that's the case—but that our effort is something *we* control, no one else. We need to own it in an uncompromising fashion.

When our team was having a bad year in 2011, part of my responsibility was to lead by example when it came to both attitude and hard work. I couldn't just stroll into the office for a few hours each day singing, "Everything is awesome!" I had to roll up my sleeves and give the same maximum effort I hoped to get from others—all without grumbling or complaining about how and why we got there.

When I've felt exhausted from the battles of life, I've reminded myself that neither people nor circumstance could keep me from continuing to give great effort. That effort hasn't always gotten me a victory, but it has allowed me to live without regret.

We all get to decide how hard we will work and how we will view our world. We own our attitude and our effort. And that's how we control our response.

TAKING CONTROL

I'd love to tell you that my attitude is always upbeat and my effort is always maxed out. But we all have bad days. The question is, what will we do with those bad days? Will they become part of a pattern that colors our life? Or will they mark a pivot toward a portrait of something better?

Think about it this way: Imagine a large whiteboard like you find in a typical conference room. Now imagine that you took an orange marker and put dots all over the white-board to represent all your bad days, starting from the left (your birth) and moving to the right until you get to today. The worse your attitude and effort was on those days and the longer you allowed the funk to last, the larger the dot.

Now, take a seat on the far side of the conference table and take a look at the whiteboard.

What's the pattern? Maybe quite a few big orange dots during those middle school and junior high years, I'm guessing. Then what?

My board certainly would have plenty of orange dots. I realized early in life, however, that leaders cast a shadow, and we have a responsibility to work through bad days quickly and transparently so that we don't pull everyone around us into a collective pit of misery. Our ability to own our attitude and effort not only is good for us, but it's good for everyone around us. And it changes what we see on that whiteboard.

Speaking of the whiteboard, go back to the one you envisioned and make some new dots, but this time let the dots represent your good days. Use multiple colors: One color for good days with your family when you were grow-ing up. Another for your good days with friends when you were in high school. Another for good days with friends when you were in college. Another for good days with your spouse and children. Another for your good days at work. Another for your good days with adult friends. And how about one for good days when you were all alone? Those are often very good days.

That whiteboard no longer looks like a carrot, does it? In fact, you hardly see the orange. Instead, you see the colorful power of your attitude and effort.

Regardless of what your board looks like, however, you can't erase it. But you can affect the picture with your next decision. And your next. And your next. You can change the view of the board by owning your attitude and effort moving forward so that they support your quest for a greater life.

TAKING ON YOUR BIGGEST COMPETITOR—YOURSELF

Motivational speaker Jim Rohn has said we're all the average of the five people we spend the most time with. There is wisdom in that message, which is why Chapter 9 is all about relationships. One relationship, however, skews the average, and that's the person we spend the most time with—ourselves.

As much as I value the men and women in my "kitchen cabinet," I am not around them all day. And as much as I value input from my wife, I often go hours and hours when she's not physically in my presence.

Me, on the other hand? I am my constant companion. I am there when I lie down, there when I get up, and there as I deal with all the joys and challenges of my day.

That makes me both my closest friend but also my biggest competitor. That competitor is always wrestling with me, and sometimes he doesn't fight fair.

When I become my own advisory, I am no longer a very good advisor or source of motivation. Because no one knows me better than me, I can focus too much on my weaknesses and my unworthiness. The more I allow those types of messages to soak in, the more they have a negative effect on my attitude and effort. I start to believe that I'm no good at all or that there's no point in trying.

To control my attitude and effort, I have found I have to recognize that sometimes the biggest obstacle in my pathway is me. I have to face that enemy and speak truth back to it. Not long ago, for instance, I got a call from a friend who had just become a member of the prestigious Augusta National Golf Club. There are only around three hundred members in this club, and it's by invitation only. Warren Buffett, Bill Gates, and Pete Coors are among the members, and former members include Dwight Eisenhower, T. Boone Pickens, and Jack Welch.

Getting into Augusta National, in other words, is a big deal. But it's especially big for blacks, who weren't invited in until 1990, and women, who couldn't become members until 2012. My friend joined the likes of Lynn Swann and Condoleezza Rice as an African American member.

I confess I felt a tinge of jealousy. I also had that thought for a second that my successes in life weren't enough.

I don't know about you, but when I start to live through someone else's lens, I never find happiness. Only disappointment. I had to retake control of my attitude and remind myself to be happy for my friend and be content in who I am and what I've accomplished in life.

We all are unique in our personalities, but I believe attitude and effort are traits we can develop, nurture, and repair if we are strategic and intentional in taking on our biggest competitor. Here are a few ways to go about it:

Embrace life's risks.

What would you do if you knew you could not fail? Would you start a new business? Take up mountain biking? Run for president? Write a book?

The fear of failure does more damage to our success than failure itself. It stops us before we even get started, so we never make the effort to pursue our dreams. But when we learn that it's OK to fall, we can take control of our attitude and give the consistent effort to overcome both the fear of failure and actual failures.

Each step I took in my career came with a risk of failure, because I was always taking on a new and bigger challenge. That meant I couldn't give fear of failure control over my attitude. I could have stayed put at American Converters. I was comfortable. There weren't many unknowns. Leaving for a job with Pepsi came with lots of unknowns. So did every move I made. But I went into them with the attitude that I was ready—not just to do the job, but to work hard doing that job and learning what I needed to know.

Often this attitude has challenged me to trust my instincts when the best choice wasn't obvious and others on my team disagreed with me. In 2015, for instance, I suggested we expand our annual leadership meeting to include everyone in the West Division who was a director or above—about five hundred people. Before, we only brought in vice presidents and up, so the change would cost a good bit of additional time and money to plan and put on.

My management team was pretty much split down the middle on the idea. About half thought it was a great idea, while the other half thought it was awful. I respected and considered the opinions of both groups but ultimately trusted my gut and took the risk of expanding.

The WD 500, the same event where Wes Moore spoke, became a wonderful success because it gave us an opportunity to align on strategies and vision, encourage each other, and let the cultural paint of our organization drip down to every level of our leadership team.

To make it happen, I had to embrace the risk with a good attitude and complete effort. I couldn't be discouraged by or angry toward those who didn't think it would work. I had to respect them, but I also had to respect my instincts. And then I had to work hard to ensure we overcame the challenges that made the idea risky.

Take the long view.

Attitude and effort aren't a one-time, short-term exercise; they require patience and a long view of the future, because there are no shortcuts to success.

I love the story of Dashrath Manjhi, who proved that with attitude and effort, you can literally move a mountain.

Manjhi was born in 1934, grew up poor in the tiny mountain village of Gehlaur, and was a member of the lowest rung in India's caste system. He was working as a farm laborer in 1959 when his wife died in an accident. That's when Manjhi resolved to cut a road through a rocky mountain ridge to give his village better access to medical care that might have saved the love of his life.

With nothing more than a hammer and chisel, Manjhi went to work. Day after day, week after week, month after month, and year after year, he spent his days in the fields and most of his spare time battling the mountain.

The locals, of course, thought he was crazy.

"When I started hammering the hill," he said, "people called me a lunatic, but that steeled my resolve."[23]

---

23 Jeremiah Jacques, "The Man Who Moved a Mountain," *The Trumpet,* April 2016, https://www.thetrumpet.com/13619-the-man-who-moved-a-mountain, last accessed July 18, 2020.

In 1982, twenty-two years after he began, Manjhi had carved a path through the rock that was 360 feet long, 30 feet wide, and in some places nearly 25 feet deep. As a result, he had shortened the distance of travel between the Atri and Wazirganj sectors of the Gaya district from thirty-four miles to about nine miles.

"Though most villagers taunted me at first," Manjhi said, "there were quite a few who lent me support later by giving me food and helping me buy my tools."[24]

A road now exists on the path he carved, and while Manjhi has since passed away, the legacy of the "Mountain Man" lives on, all because he patiently persevered with attitude and effort.

Feed the positive, starve the negative.

The things you feed and nurture are the things that will grow stronger. What you put inside of you has everything to do with what comes out of you, and that goes for your mind and soul as well as your body. So a key to owning your attitude and effort is to feed them with the things that will make them strong and starve them of things that make them weak.

Personally, I start my days early with prayer and reflection. I visualize how things will look if my goals and dreams are achieved. I listen to podcasts and read things that are encouraging and that give me practical ideas about how to be a better husband, father, and leader.

My reflection time also always includes counting my blessings. It might sound like a cliché, but I assure you it works.

24 BS Web Team, "'Mountain Man' comes alive on the silver screen," *Business Standard*, July 14, 2015, https://www.business-standard.com/article/beyond-business/mountain-man-comes-alive-on-the-silver-screen-115071400525_1.html, last accessed July 18, 2020.

When things are going well, counting my blessings keeps me humble, thankful, and motivated to keep working hard and to acknowledge others who have helped me achieve my goals.

If I'm having a down day, it never fails to improve my spirits, and it gives me fresh control over my attitude and my effort. When I remember that I've been blessed with a wonderful wife, that we had a child late in life, that we both came from broken homes but are breaking that generational curse, that I have a great job, that...well, I could keep going on and on, but it doesn't take long before I realize I'd have to be an idiot to complain about anything.

When I say we need to starve our minds of the negative, by the way, I realize that we can't ignore reality, and sometimes reality is rather negative. Making gratitude a daily choice doesn't change reality. It doesn't eliminate my exhaustion, and it won't make your trials or troubles disappear. But it will help you stay uncompromising in your attitude and effort. When your mind is full of what's possible and what's good, you can take a positive view of the most negative realities. Then you feel far more eager to do the hard work of making things better.

That's how Blake Anderson said he got through the most difficult trial in his life. Anderson was the head football coach at Arkansas State University when he lost his wife, Wendy, to cancer just prior to the 2019 season. She was only forty-nine years old. Less than a year later, his father died as well.

"I tell my players all the time: attitude is a choice," Anderson said. "I had to choose that I'm going to be grateful for the things I have and not spend my time wallowing in pity for the things I've lost. And at the end of the day, my dad and Wendy are in a better place."[25]

And, in fact, I also realize that the worst times in my life helped shaped me for future success. They taught me something valuable because I was committed to failing forward. So whatever it is that has me down, it's something I'll look back on later as a blessing.

GETTING STARTED

The hard work of taking on your biggest competitor starts with carving out space in your life to make it happen.

In Chapter 5 on the learning lab pathway, I mentioned that I regularly get up in the predawn hours to give myself time for intentional reflection. This is one of the many areas where the pathways crisscross, because this habit also is critical preparation for owning my attitude and effort. The right attitude and effort set me up to make the most of the learning lab and to have a productive day.

It's in that space that we make a choice about what we will try to control and how we will go about owning our attitude and effort. The key choices are ours alone. We look at the options, make a decision, and live with the consequences. Others might influence us, but we own our decision.

Will we control those things we can actually control, or will we yield them to the world around us? Will we sit and sulk our way through the day, or will we take charge of our emotions and our actions?

---

25   George Stoia, "Living with grief: After losing his wife and father, Arkansas State Coach Blake Anderson endured the toughest year of his life," *Arkansas Democrat-Gazette*, August 19, 2020.

To make the best choices, we have to find time to be still and listen. We have to dig deep within ourselves without distractions so we can put on the armor that allows us to feed a positive mindset, fail forward, exercise patience, make sure we are living our life and not someone else's, and count our blessings.

When we try to control the things we can't control, we eventually get frustrated and we often become overly demanding, no fun to be around, and less effective in accomplishing the things we want to see accomplished.

When we make a conscious decision to control only that which we can control, our attitude and effort, we can enjoy the journey wherever it takes us, even if—no, make that even *when*—it takes us places we never expected to go. As I'll explain in the next chapter, the straight line to success is actually crooked. And if we don't own our attitude and effort on the crooked roads of life, we'll find ourselves going off a cliff.

Chapter 8

Pathway 6—Navigate Uncertainty

The straight line to success is actually crooked.

MY VIEW OF MY FUTURE began shifting in a new direction during my sophomore year of college. There was no defining moment, at least not that I can identify. When it comes to weighty decisions, my mind is more like a Crock-Pot than a microwave. So all I know is that at some time in the early 1980s, I realized there might just be a curve in my straight path to success.

I arrived at Indiana University with the clear belief that I would be the next Bryant Gumbel. I loved sports, but I wasn't good enough to make a career out of shooting hoops. And I had thrived in speech class in high school, thanks to the encouragement and support of Alice Goodrum. Add all that up and the sportscaster gig seemed like the ideal career.

Gumbel was the perfect role model. NBC, ABC, and CBS were still the Big Three when it came to national sports broadcasts, and Gumbel regularly worked NBC's broadcasts for Major League Baseball, college basketball, and the National Football League. There weren't many black sportscasters in the 1970s, but there he was on the biggest stage of all.

Drawing inspiration from his success, as well from Ms. Goodrum and my love for sports, I majored in journalism, wrote for the school newspaper (the *Indiana Daily Student*), and did the radio broadcasts for a few non-revenue sports to gain experience. It was only a matter of time before I would join Gumbel in the studio or broadcast booth—or that I would replace him!

It wasn't long, however, before I realized I was more in love with the outcome than the work it would take to achieve that outcome.

When we commit to a dream, it's easy to slide into a bubble where we stubbornly refuse to listen to anyone or anything that challenges our view of the world we want to create. There's a difference, however, between being undeterred by critics and obstacles when we're on the right path and blindly driving off a cliff because we're too stubborn or arrogant to read the warning signs.

Part of being "radically responsible" is knowing when to shift our direction, sometimes in significant ways. This adds an essential element of balance to an uncompromising life. If we're fiercely independent, scrappy, and undistracted in pursuit of the wrong things or for the wrong reasons, we can spend years barreling down the road of regret.

I was committed to the path of sports journalism. That was the dream. But I also was constantly gathering information from my experiences and from the people I respected. I knew there was a great deal about my dream career that I didn't know and that I needed to learn. So while I wouldn't let others push me away from my dream or define my dream, I was open-minded enough to let good information shape my decisions.

On the one hand, I enjoyed the journalism path because it kept me connected to sports, I met interesting people, and it was a great way to experience and get to know Indiana University.

On the other hand, the professors at IU were realistic when it came to painting a picture of what it took to reach the higher levels of success in sports journalism. Gumbel was at NBC by the time he was twenty-eight years old, but he was an exception. Landing a job at a major market, much less a national network, typically took years in the trenches. My degree would likely get me a job in a small market, where I could expect to cover high school sports and bring home less than $10,000 a year. Even if I did well, it would be a long climb up the ladder to larger markets and larger salaries.

Looking around campus, meanwhile, I noticed that many of the kids I considered "successful"—including my closest friend, Stanford "Lukie" Miller—were majoring in business. So I decided to minor in business with the idea that those classes would prepare me for life and give me additional options after graduation. I really enjoyed those classes and realized I was more interested in building busi-nesses than writing about them (or sports or anything else).

Business, I discovered, suited my natural instincts and talents for things like organizing, problem-solving, and leading. It also paid better. Much better. So, as Bryant Gumbel was transitioning from sports to *The Today Show*, I reset my sights on a career in the corporate world. The road to success would still be long and difficult, I realized, but I saw far more opportunities for using my gifts to achieve what was then a huge driving force in my life—escaping poverty as quickly as possible!

When the recruiters came to campus during my senior year, I mostly visited the ones with opportunities in sales. I landed three job offers and took one that sent me to New Jersey to sell medical supplies in the New York City area. They offered me $21,500 a year—double what I figured to make in an entry-level journalism job—and it seemed like I'd struck it rich.

As it turned out, I never had a job where a journalism degree was a requirement. I learned things in my journalism training, however, that have helped me throughout my career in business, because, as we've already discussed, life is a learning lab and everything we experience has value if we look for ways to apply it to our circumstances.

In journalism, for instance, I learned how to tell a story in a succinct, organized way. The discipline of highlighting what was truly important without rambling on and on helped me communicate more effectively, whether it was in one-on-one situations or while delivering speeches or presentations.

Journalism courses also developed my natural curiosity to ask questions and learn new things. And they taught me how to practice active listening so I not only heard the story I was being told but the one that wasn't being told as well. By listening closely, I learned to go a layer or two deeper to find the real story, which often gave me an edge when it came to information and insights.

Most people, even those who find a calling early in life and never veer from it, have twists and turns in their road to success. It might look like they followed a straight line, but if you look more closely, you'll see it was actually crooked.

I never went back to sports journalism, but my career path still wasn't as straight as it might first appear. If you look at it from a distance, you see a guy who graduated college, took a job in sales, steadily worked his way up the corporate ladder, and eventually earned a spot as a top-level executive in a large corporation. You already know it wasn't that simple.

My journey definitely has taken the roads less trav-elled—a broken road from Florida, through Georgia, to the inner-city streets of Indiana, and then all over the United States. I've worked in sales, marketing, operations, and management for a hospital supply company, a beverage company, a consumer products company, and multiple cable companies.

It took me a couple of tries just to write down all four-teen moves I have made in my adult life—from college to New Jersey to Chicago to Michigan back to Chicago to Connecticut to Virginia to New York City to Atlanta back to New York City back to Connecticut back to Chicago to Atlanta to California and, finally (I think!), to Denver. Whew! I should have invested in a moving company somewhere along the way.

Barbita and I met and married when we both were in Virginia, and she joined me for every twist and turn there-after. She had a successful career in marketing with IBM, but she agreed to find another job when my work took us to New York. She found a new job again when we moved to Atlanta. Then in Connecticut. When I got my next new job offer, this one back in Chicago, she decided to pour her energy and talents into different types of opportunities.

I am thankful for her sacrifices and for her ability to find self-worth in areas that don't bring a traditional paycheck.

She finds joy in supporting my career, in volunteering, and especially in being a mother. While that role came later, it truly is her calling in life. And think about how crooked the path to that role was for her. Indeed, I've learned a lot about navigating uncertainty from the examples she has set throughout our life together.

THE ROLE OF UNCERTAINTY

Once we discover that the straight path to success is actually crooked, we quickly encounter another reality: there's a ton of uncertainty on a crooked path!

When the path takes twists and turns, a scrappy and undistracted mindset and an unwavering commitment to our why all become vitally important, because, again, control is an illusion. Everyone's life includes uncertainty. We often have no idea what's around the next corner, and sometimes what we think we'll find is totally different from what's actually there. We chart our courses, but plans change. Sometimes we choose to change; at other times, change comes despite our greatest efforts. Markets crash. Pandemics linger. Accidents occur. And people—the great X factor—do things we never expected that force us to pivot.

When my parents got married, I'm sure they both had a rosy vision for their future. I'm confident it didn't involve alcoholism, divorce, a move that would take their children hundreds of miles from their father, or a job for my mother cleaning rooms at an economy motel.

As the marriage deteriorated, my mother began making more and more decisions on the highway of uncertainty, and it led her to a very different future than she originally envisioned for her family. I can only imagine the trepidation she must have experienced as she watched the mile markers roll by on that bus ride from Georgia through Nashville and Louisville and on to Indianapolis. Greyhound navigated the highways for nearly nine hours to get us to our new home, but then she would have to navigate uncertainty for years to come.

The prospect of that uncertainty challenged and inspired her. It held the potential to knock her down and keep her down, but it also held within it the opportunities for a better life.

As humans, we have something of a love-hate relationship with uncertainty.

Neuroscientists have found that we crave certainty. It's a reward our brains seek for avoiding dangers associated with uncertainty. David Rock, director of the NeuroLeadership Institute and the author of *Your Brain at Work*, says uncertainty triggers a chemical response that causes us to fear what we don't fully know or understand.

"Your brain detects something is wrong, and your ability to focus on other issues diminishes," Rock says. "Your brain doesn't like uncertainty—it's like a type of pain, something to be avoided. Certainty on the other hand feels rewarding, and we tend to steer toward it, even when it might be better for us to remain uncertain."[26]

While we crave certainty, there's also an allure to uncertainty. Motivational speaker Tony Robbins says six universal needs drive all human behavior, and while certainty is

26   David Rock, "A Hunger for Certainty: Your brain craves certainty and avoids uncertainty like it's pain," *Psychology Today*, October 25, 2009, https://www.psychologytoday.com/us/blog/your-brain-work/200910/hunger-certainty, last accessed July 23, 2020.

one of them, uncertainty is another.[27] We feel a pull into the unknown. It's the curiosity we talked about earlier, the desire to learn and experience new things.

Yet even when we are drawn toward uncertainty—when we long for variety or a discovery that comes with trying something totally new—we pursue it with a goal of understanding it or overcoming it. The thrill of the unknown, in other words, is satisfied by transforming it into something we know. We love a surprise, Robbins points out, so long as it's a surprise we want. Otherwise we call it a problem. The challenge, therefore, becomes making the most of uncertainty—to navigate it well so that we end up where we really want to go.

A MAP FOR THE CROOKED ROAD

This pathway is called "navigate uncertainty," not "avoid uncertainty." We can't avoid it, but we can navigate it and learn from it along the way. How we navigate the uncertainties of life goes a long way toward shaping our opportunities for success, and I've identified a few uncompromising best practices that have been key parts of my personal map:

Get in the game.

When I was growing up, I didn't even know there was a game, much less that I should get in it.

No one came up to me and said, "You look like a nice kid. Let me tell you about the game. Here's a map to the

---

27   The others, he says, are significance, connection/love, growth, and contribution. See "Do You Need to Feel Significant," tonyrobbins.com, *https://www.tonyrobbins.com/mind-meaning/do-you-need-to-feel-significant/*, last accessed July 23, 2020.

arena where you'll find the game. And here's a ticket to get in. And here's a bat, ball, and glove. And a rulebook. And I'll be glad to go with you and explain how it all works. I'll put you through some drills to teach you all the skills you need. And if you have questions, just call time-out and come check with me."

The game—and I'm talking about life, not baseball, basketball, or hockey—is a great big stadium full of uncertainty. The rules change all the time. The field isn't always level. The bleachers often are full of your opponent's fans. And there are times when you have no coaches or teammates volunteering to help you along the way.

I'm not saying I had no help—you know that's not true—but ultimately it was up to me to find the game, learn the rules of the game, and, most importantly, get in the game.

Millions of people have disadvantages to overcome in life. Society needs to do its part to make the rules more consistent and the field more level, but we can't stay on the sidelines waiting for that to happen. We can't navigate the uncertainties of life from the sidelines. We have to get creative and figure out a way to get into the game—through a side door, up from the basement entry, or by cutting a hole in the roof. Whatever it takes. Get in the game, or this much is certain: you'll never win.

I have done a pretty good job of getting in the game, but I also missed some opportunities to put this pathway into practice. For instance, because I had done a good job as a manager for my high school basketball team, Coach Cline reached out to Indiana Coach Bob Knight and suggested he put me to work as a manager for the Hoosiers. I interviewed with the coaches, including Coach Knight.

They didn't have an opening at the time, but they told me to stay in touch.

That's where it ended, because that's where I let it end. I didn't follow up. I didn't become that annoying student who kept showing up until they gave me the job. I let the uncertainty of a "not now" become a "not ever."

Indiana won two Big Ten titles and the 1981 NCAA championship while I was in college, and I might have been a part of those teams if I had navigated a little uncertainty by getting myself in the game.

Not being a manager for IU basketball isn't a huge regret in my life, but I definitely see it as an opportunity I missed out on for no other reason than I didn't make the effort to make it happen. And I'll never know how that experience might have shaped my life.

If we don't figure out ways to get in the game, we won't get the opportunity to navigate opportunities that lead us to a fulfilling life.

Stay in the game.

It doesn't matter who you are, where you came from, or what advantages you had or lacked along the way—you personally have to decide how committed you'll be to navigating the uncertainties of life. Because getting in the game isn't enough. You have to stay in it. Yeah, it is exhausting at times, but it is better to deal with exhaustion than to accept defeat.

Staying in the game is more challenging for some than others, but an uncompromising mindset requires a no-excuses approach to uncertainty. When I didn't make the basketball team in high school, I had to find a way to stay in the game as a manager. When I didn't have the money to attend IU, I had to find a way to stay in the game by enrolling in programs designed to help first-generation college students. When I was fired, I had to find a way to prove I could make the most of the next opportunity.

This pathway, by the way, isn't just for those who come from a single-parent household, who faced discrimination, who didn't have much money growing up, or who were saddled with any number of other disadvantages. I've known plenty of people who were born into privilege but never really stayed in the game. They had all the advantages when it came to education, money, and opportunity, but they abused those privileges, squandered their opportunities, or didn't full take advantage of what they were given.

One friend of mine in particular stands out in my memory. He wasn't from a super wealthy family, but you'd probably consider his parents middle class. They had college degrees, good jobs, and high expectations for their son. He made good grades, attended college, and earned a degree. He had plenty of connections to help him land a well-paying job on a stable career path. Instead, he drifted into the drug culture, became a dealer, and has spent much of his life taking advantage of the vulnerable rather than helping them.

I've also known people who got in the game early but didn't stick with it. They were highfliers for a time but then dropped out when faced with obstacles and uncertainties. They lacked an unwavering commitment to excellence and to their fight.

Others, like George Carruthers, were born into certain advantages, worked hard, embraced uncertainty, and turned their lives into something even bigger and better.

Carruthers' father had earned a degree from the University of Illinois and was working as a civil engineer in

Ohio when George was born in 1939. George's uncle also attended UI, where he earned a PhD and went on to success as a writer and photographer.

George was twelve when his father died and his mother moved the family back to the south side of Chicago. He had shown an interest in astronomy, building his own telescopes to look at the night skies in rural Ohio, but he easily could have drifted down a path of mediocrity after moving to the inner city. Instead, he began winning science fairs and spent much of his spare time visiting museums, libraries, and the Adler Planetarium.

Still, when he arrived at the University of Illinois, he found himself less prepared for the academic rigor of a university than many of the other students. He could have seen that as a roadblock that would limit or even end his journey; instead, it was just another twist in the road.

"I went to a mostly black high school and suddenly went to a mostly white university in which I was competing not with inner city kids like myself, but guys from the suburbs," he once recalled. "I remember that because my mathematics background in high school was not adequate, not because I got bad grades, but because they just didn't have the courses that were required. I had to go to summer school the first year that I was in college and make up mathematics courses."[28]

Carruthers said he never experienced overt discrimination while in college, but neither was he invited to socialize or join the study clubs with white students. "Not that they would prevent you from coming," he said, "but they just don't invite you."

---

28   David DeVorkin, "Oral Histories: George Carruthers," American Institute of Physics, August 18, 1992, *https://www.aip.org/history-programs/niels-bohr-library/oral-histories/32485#top*, last accessed November 10, 2020.

He stayed focused on his prize, however, and eventually earned multiple degrees, including a PhD in aeronautical and astronomical engineering. Then he went to work for the US Naval Research Laboratory in Washington, DC, and he earned patents for several space-related inventions, including the ultraviolet camera/spectrograph NASA used on Apollo 16 in 1972. He was inducted into the National Inventors Hall of Fame, and he was an advocate for getting African Americans more involved in science and technology careers.

Carruthers didn't squander the advantages he was given. He used what he had to get in the game and play to win. That's my hope for my son—he was born into certain advantages, but he still has to get in the game and stay in the game.

Face your doubts (and doubters).

One of the reasons we get out of the game is because we give in to our doubts.

There are moments of uncertainty when it seems like everyone is telling us that we can't do whatever it is we've set out to do. They tell us to stop or turn back or take an easier road, and they plant (or water) seeds of doubt in our minds.

The easiest thing to do with these doubts is surrender to them. But, as Bertrand Russell pointed out way back in 1933, it's usually the wrong people who are waving the white flag. "The fundamental cause of the trouble is that in the modern world the stupid are cocksure while the intelligent are full of doubt," Russell wrote.[29]

---

29 Bertrand Russell, "The Triumph of Stupidity," *New York American*, May 10, 1933; collected in *Mortals and Others: American Essays* (New York: Routledge, 2009 edition).

The "stupid," to use Russell's word, don't want the facts to get in the way of their good stories, so they command the room by making noise that drowns out competing voices. The intelligent prefer to think things through, which leads to the humbling reality that they don't have all the answers. The humility is good, but we can't allow it to keep us from the truths that move us in the right direction.

Shakespeare called doubts "traitors" that keep us from winning something good because we are afraid to even make the attempt.[30] When we doubt ourselves, it's usually because we fear failure. When others doubt us, it often is because they fear something from our success.

To navigate uncertainty, we have to face those fears by speaking truth into them. Confronting our doubts, whether they come from within us or from outsiders, might cause us to course correct, but it won't lead us toward surrender. In fact, facing these doubts gives us a "good chip" to put on our shoulder that motivates us to prove our doubters wrong.

When I overheard family members telling my mother her sons would never amount to anything, their doubts became my motivational chip. When I was passed over by teachers or supervisors who, typically without saying it out loud, sent a message of "you're not good enough," their doubts became my motivational chip. If I had never faced those doubters, I never would have gotten beyond the uncertainty they raised in my mind.

And a good fear is what motivated me to get back in the game after I was fired. I was afraid of the uncertainty that stood before me, but I faced my doubts, put myself

30 William Shakespeare, *Measure for Measure*, 1603, http://shakespeare.mit.edu/measure/full.html, last accessed August 12, 2021.

out there, and fully invested in my future. I didn't just dip a toe into the water, either; I dove in the deep end.

Why? I had a good fear of failure. I didn't want to be poor again, but even more than that, I didn't want to let my family down, I didn't want to let my race down, and I didn't want to let myself down. I used those fears to overcome my doubts and to get me back in the game.

Be certain in your uncertainty.

When I read details about the life of Abraham Lincoln, I am amazed at what he accomplished—not just that he led the United States through the most turbulent times in its history and brought an end to slavery, but that he ever became president at all.

Lincoln, as you probably know, was born in a one-room log cabin in Kentucky and raised in poverty in rural Indiana before moving to Illinois as a young man. His father was illiterate, and his mother died when he was nine years old. But he learned to read (thanks to his stepmother), worked hard, and impressed people with his sharp mind and integrity.

It soon became clear he would do well for himself, but his career in politics didn't get off to a very good start. In his first bid for public office, Lincoln finished eighth in a field of thirteen candidates. He bounced back and won four terms in the state legislature and a seat in the US House of Representatives, only to lose when he ran for the US Senate—twice.

While Lincoln was known for his wit and humor, scholars have concluded that he also suffered from bouts of depression for much of his life. His wife is believed to have had bipolar disorder, and three of the four sons born to the couple died in childhood.

Add to all of that the fact that he had to turn the course of a nation that in many quarters had no desire to change and it's clear that Lincoln's road to success was as crooked as the lines in his face.

In all of his uncertainty, however, Lincoln always managed to remember his purpose, and it was his purpose that pulled him through what had to be exhausting periods of his life. When, like Lincoln, we find our fight and keep our eye on that prize, we strengthen ourselves for the uncertainty that threatens to knock us off our course.

Being certain of our values and sure of our why are most important, in fact, when the world around us gets dark and we are struggling in our personal exhaustion.

I mentioned previously that getting fired helped me find my fight, but my life wasn't transformed with the flash of a lightning bolt. The next few years in particular were fraught with uncertainty. I moved to Chicago and began figuring things out. But just as I began to realize the specific changes I needed to make, I moved to Avon, Connecticut, as a regional operations director for American Hospital Supply.

This was a new role in a different division of the company, and I was stepping outside of my comfort zone. My mentor and sponsor, Darnell Martin, was releasing me back into the wild, and I was trying to regain my confidence and rebalance my life after an epic failure. I felt like a kid on that first bike ride without the training wheels—eager and excited, but nervous and scared. I wobbled along, fell several times, and wondered if I'd ever get it right.

By that time, however, I was certain that I was on the right path and that I had found a worthy fight—using my leadership roles to serve others. Falling wasn't fun, but

I could see it as part of the process. I was certain in my uncertainty, and that allowed me to navigate my way forward with a scrappy and undistracted mindset.

Drop anchors for the storms.

Unless we're uncompromising in our approach, uncertainty will rule us, and we will end up tossed about in the middle of the ocean. That's why we have to be anchored to our values and unwavering in our commitment to our why.

Through the years, I've spent a good bit of time thinking about my approach to life, leadership, and management. I now know that woven into my uncompromising mindset is a series of core values that guide the way I want to think and act: faith, family, hard work and attitude, teamwork, fairness, and not being a victim. I have similar lists that outline things like my aspirational leadership qualities—inspirational, consistent, tough but fair, strategic, focused, and employee-first.

I regularly revisit those values and use them as filters for navigating the uncertainties of my life. They have served me well for decades, but they took on a greater significance in December 2012 when two things happened. First, our son was born. Second, I wrote a paper I titled, "Vision 2020: My Life, Making a Difference." The two are related, of course. Having a son challenged me to take my values and map out a plan for my future.

In addition to the vision document, I also now have a notebook in my home office titled, "Steve White Strategic Plan 2020." It's the sequel to "Steve White Strategic Plan 2019," which was born out of "Steve White Strategic Plan 2018." And by the time you read this book, I'll be well into "Steve White Strategic Plan 2022" or some other, newer edition. You get the idea.

These notebooks have about a dozen tabbed sections filled with pages where I've written down what I am planning to do and how I'm planning to get it done. The simple discipline of writing down our goals improves our chances of achieving them by as much as 42 percent, according to some researchers.[31]

My plan anchors me to values, points me toward my why, and guides me through the inevitable uncertainties. But an uncompromising life is not inflexible or stubborn—otherwise I'd be a sportscaster.

Writing out a plan is part of how I gather and process information so that I don't navigate uncertainty in ignorance. I want to absorb as much information as possible and use it to guide me in wisdom. Then I can adjust, sometimes in significant ways, but I can base those adjustments on good information that allows me to stay true to my values and fighting for my why.

Make stops along the road.

The flip side of being a planner is that at times I'm too future focused. It's good to look to the horizon, but I can get so busy looking ahead that I miss what is right in front of me. When navigating uncertainty, I've had to make an intentional effort to stop from time to time, orient myself, learn from and appreciate where I am, and then chart my way forward.

It was an uncompromising desire to live out this principle that led to my retirement as president of Comcast West. I reached a point where I felt working a few more years no longer was worth missing out of the experiences I

---

31   Mary Morrissey, "The Power of Writing Down Your Goals and Dreams," HuffPost, last modified December 6, 2017, *https://www.huffpost.com/entry/the-power-of-writing-down_b_12002348?guccounter=1*, last accessed July 30, 2020.

routinely missed with my wife and son. I had worked hard to put myself in a position to do some different things with my time, and I decided to do them while I was still young enough and healthy enough to enjoy them.

Stopping during the good times allows us to appreciate the moment so we can more fully enjoy the journey. We can reflect on how we got there—the uncertainty we navigated, the people who helped us, and the lessons we learned. With humility and gratitude, we're better positioned to make the most of our next move.

The certainty of uncertainty, of course, also ensures that we will experience hard times and failures along the crooked road. We will get disoriented and lost. We will get in a few wrecks. There will be detours. We will get laid off or fired. We will go through a divorce. We will find ourselves homeless. We will fall into an addiction. Our business will fail. We will get sued. A coworker or business partner will stab us in the back. We will get sick—or, worse, someone we love will get sick.

The greatest uncertainty I've experienced in my life happened in 2016. Barbita had some outpatient surgery on a Friday, and two days later, we realized there was an unexpected complication.

I was playing golf that Sunday when my mother-in-law who was visiting us called and said Barbita had passed out and been rushed to the hospital. We later learned that her lung had been nicked during the outpatient surgery and she had been bleeding internally.

Barbita was in the hospital for eight days, and so was I. We had someone who could stay with Stevie, so I never went home. I stayed by her side the entire time, and I'm pretty sure I called, emailed, or texted everyone we had ever known to ask them to pray for my wife.

There were several days when I thought Barbita might not make it, and I wasn't thinking about my work or retirement or any of our plans for the future. I was just hoping we'd have one more day together. And then one more. And one more.

Thankfully, she recovered, but I don't think I could have navigated that uncertainty if I hadn't been uncompromising about pulling off the road and focusing entirely on her.

When something unexpected and unpleasant happens and the way forward isn't clear, it's easy to stay lost, to stay disoriented, to stay wrecked, to never get off the detour and back on the right road. If we stop, seek advice, count our blessings, and don't rush back into life, we can learn from it and even find joy in those moments. Then the bad can be turned into something good.

Getting lost? Having wrecks? Those things are inevitable.

Staying lost or living in the clouds of inactivity? That's a choice.

THE ARENA OF UNCERTAINTY

In the spring of 1910, Theodore Roosevelt made a stop in Paris as part of a post-presidential tour. He had spent a year hunting in Africa, and he was attending events in places like Cairo, Berlin, Naples, and Paris before returning to the United States.

The title of his speech for the audience in Paris was "Citizenship in a Republic," but now it is better known as "The Man in the Arena," and it would become the most quoted talk of his career.

You've probably seen it in a frame on someone's desk—in fact, it is in a frame on my desk, thanks to a former executive who once worked with me. Maybe you can even recite its most famous line—"It is not the critic who counts..."—or other significant passages.

It has stood the test of time not just because it is poetic, although it is poetic, but because it so poignantly describes what it means to battle the uncertainties of life—to get in the game, to be certain in your uncertainty, to stay anchored to your values and your why, to make stops and make the most of those stops, and to face your doubts and fears and use them to your advantage.

Even if you've read it before, don't waste this opportunity to read it again. And again.

It is not the critic who counts; not the man who points out how the strong man stumbles or where the doer of deeds could have done them better. The credit belongs to the man who is actually in the arena, whose face is marred by dust and sweat and blood; who strives valiantly; who errs, who comes short again and again, because there is no effort without error and shortcoming; but who does actually strive to do the deeds; who knows the great enthusiasms, the great devotions; who spends himself in a worthy cause; who at the best knows in the end the triumph of high achievement, and who at the worst, if he fails, at least fails while daring greatly, so that his place shall never be with those cold and timid souls who neither know victory nor defeat.[32]

---

32   Theodore Roosevelt, "Citizenship in a Republic," Sorbonne, Paris, April 23, 1910.

Soak that in and apply it to your journey. The pathway of uncertainty isn't easy, but the rewards of navigating it well are worth the risks and the effort, because the crooked paths lead you to the most meaningful places in the arena.

Chapter 9

Pathway 7—Commit to Road-Dog Relationships

Making deposits always yields big dividends.

I'VE NEVER BEEN ONE TO go looking for trouble, but trouble has found me from time to time. And one night, it found me at a skating rink.

In the late 1970s and early 1980s, roller-skating was a popular pastime for teenagers, and my friends and I often headed to the rink when we were in college. We would lace up the rented skates and race across the concrete floor as strobe lights flashed to the beats of the blaring music.

Pool tables, foosball tables, and a few arcade games competed for our time and money when we took a break from skating. And we would socialize around the snack bar, where the guys tried to impress the girls with our perceived wit and charm.

Most of these evenings were uneventful, but one night I did or said something that sparked a disagreement with another guy. The details are lost to me, but I'm pretty sure it involved a girl. This much I do remember: he was signifi-

cantly bigger than me, and he seemed eager to demonstrate what I suspected were his superior warrior skills.

As the battle evolved from words (where I was confident I had the advantage) toward fists (where I was confident I was a bit outmatched), divine intervention arrived in
the form of Lukie, a.k.a. Stanford Miller.

I've mentioned Lukie a few times already. He is my close
friend and was a cofounder of the group we called Unique,
Inc. He's not a particularly big guy—maybe five foot ten
and 170 pounds back in our college days—but he came
flying into the picture in my defense. He didn't take the
other guy down, but let's just say he brought new energy
to the conversation, and the odds immediately shifted
in my favor.

Emboldened by this show of support, I stood my ground
with much more confidence. Mr. Tough Guy continued
to talk a good game, but he no longer showed the same
passion for a fight. Eventually, he backed away, we backed
away, and that was the end of it.

Lukie came to my rescue without needing an invitation
or explanation for one simple reason: he was my road dog.

Now, I realize that's an unusual term to describe a close
friend, but it's one I latched onto many years ago because
it was common in the neighborhood where I grew up. I
like the image of a couple of dogs traveling down the road
together. They own nothing. They often feel like the world is
conspiring against them. But they are undeterred because
they have one thing that matters—each other. No matter
what happens, they know they won't have to face it alone.

For me, road dogs embody at least four characteristics.
One, they know you as well as you know yourself, sometimes better. Two, they are transparent, so you know who

they really are, how they feel, and what they think. This means they tell you what you need to hear, not just what you want to hear. Three, they care about you unconditionally, so their tough love doesn't come with judgments. And, four, you seldom have to ask each other for favors because you each respond to the other's needs before a request can be made.

OK, maybe there's a fifth characteristic: a road dog will jump into a fight without asking questions—at least that was the case with Lukie! He had no idea why I was in trouble, and he didn't waste time asking. He just responded to what he could clearly see was my need, even when he knew it might cost him a bloody lip.

I'm not suggesting that fighting is the answer to solving conflicts, of course, but I can tell you that we all need a few road dogs in our lives. We need people we trust and can count on implicitly and who trust and can count on us— relationships that are real, not just surface level, and that create a shared value in our shared journeys through life.

When we were in college, Lukie and I intentionally went against the grain by not joining a fraternity. This marked us as social outcasts, so we had to work together to earn respect and overcome the consequences of our decision. That was the reason we created Unique, Inc. We could call each other at any time, day or night, because of the tight bond that defined our relationship.

That bond included encouragement when the exhaustions of life were weighing us down, as well as tough love and accountability when we weren't living up to the high standards we had set for ourselves. We saw the greatness in each other, and we were uncompromising in our commitment to help each other bring that greatness out. That's what road dogs do.

MY ROCKY PATHWAY

My definition of "uncompromising" includes the words "fiercely independent," but that doesn't mean we always go it alone. Deep, meaningful road-dog relationships are essential to a life well lived. They enrich us in innumerable ways, some practical and measurable, but also in ways that are as difficult to explain as the joy we feel watching a picturesque sunset.

We can never have too many of these relationships, but the number isn't what's important. Some people have dozens, while others have a few—but those few are extraordinarily powerful. What matters more is that we invest our very best into *all of our relationships* and capitalize on the opportunities to make the most of them so that we can get the most of our uncompromising approach to life.

Barbita and I are knitted together at a soul level, and we share an intimacy that's unique and reserved for marriage. There also are a few men whom I consider lifelong road-dog buddies—Ron Singletary, Teddy Snowden, Lukie, and my brothers, Anthony, Linton, and Keith. If any of them called tonight in need of help, I'd be on the next flight out.

Looking back, however, I confess that I didn't always fully invest in some relationships, and therefore I've missed out on far too many opportunities to have more road dogs in my life.

That's partly because my mother raised me and my brothers with an us-against-the-world mentality. She told us—often, I might add—that we had to stick together and that we couldn't expect help from anyone else. It was up to us to make our way. No one else. This helped us develop an independent streak that has served us well over the years, but that same mentality has caused me to wade slowly into the deeper waters of trust when other people are involved.

That doesn't mean I don't value relationships or that I struggle to develop friendships. For more than thirty years, my fight has revolved around creating a table of prosperity where everyone can participate, succeed, and enjoy life. I can't accomplish that without interacting effectively with people. I really enjoy listening to other people and learning about them and from them, and I've never had trouble sharing the surface-level stories of my life.

Routine interpersonal relationships, in other words, aren't an issue (the angry guy at the skating rink was a long-ago exception). But when it comes to inviting people into my world in ways that require deep transparency, authenticity, and trust, the path gets a bit rocky. These relationships don't come as naturally. I look for roadblocks, and if I can't find them, I tend to create them.

I'm pretty good at conditional trust. When I meet someone new, I'll give them the benefit of the doubt and extend trust based on what I know about them or what I've been told about them. But at the same time, I admit, I am also looking for confirmation that my trust was well placed. Alarm bells go off for me, for instance, when someone asks for a favor. I'm not talking about simple things like *Could you pass the salt?* or *Can I borrow your ink pen?* I'm talking about favors that feel presumptuous because they exceed the investments they've made in our relationship.

This is certainly subjective, but most of us can tell when another person is self-serving—when they view the relationship based mainly on what they can get from us so that it benefits them. It's hard for me to fully trust those types of people, because I find myself constantly questioning their motives.

Even when the other person isn't self-serving, however, it doesn't take very long to hit a thick wall that represents where my trust ends. It's not that they've done something to betray my trust; it's just that I am slow to open up about my personal fears and problems. I don't talk much, for instance, about the exhaustion that comes from my black experience. It's taken a bit of coaxing from others to get me to write about it in this book. But potential road dogs need that type of information and insight to help me grow.

As I think about my missed opportunities, my first response is to point out the challenges that come with frequent career moves. I would show up for a new job and dive headfirst into the work. I'd get to know coworkers and a few other people, but my main focus was on work and my wife. With long hours and travel, other relationships seldom went beyond the basics. And it seemed like if they did begin to develop more depth, a new opportunity would pop up, and I'd be off to the next city. Consequently, I left behind lots of acquaintances, but not many real road-dog friends.

While all of that is true, it's also a convenient excuse to cover the fact that I've failed to do the hard work of nurturing more road-dog relationships. Even worse, I've allowed petty disagreements and perceived slights to derail what could have been—and should have been—deep friendships.

At one point in my journey, for instance, I became good friends with a neighbor who was about my age and who shared many of my interests. He and I frequently played golf together. Barbita and I spent time socially with him and his wife. We watched their kids when they went out on dates. And he and I often talked through the challenges of life. But there were times when my ego told me the relationship was one-sided—that I was giving more than I was getting, even when that wasn't the case or when it should not have mattered. I allowed that to weaken my view of the friendship, which, of course, weakened the relationship.

A few years after we moved away, Barbita and I had a lengthy layover while flying through the city where our friends lived. We arranged to have dinner with them, but he canceled about an hour before we were supposed to meet. He gave no explanation. He just shot us a text saying he couldn't make it.

If I had done a better job nurturing the relationship, maybe he would have told me what was going on. Perhaps I would have asked—or trusted our friendship enough to believe he would have told me if I needed to know. Instead, I took the cancellation personally. Rather than giving him the benefit of the doubt, I jumped to conclusions and made assumptions that allowed seeds of anger and bitterness to take root in my heart.

Unfortunately, I can easily think of seven or eight relationships that could have been more significant but aren't because I either didn't nurture them and/or because my selfishness or pride got in the way of their success. That's a loss for me. Maybe it's also a loss for those other men, but it's definitely a loss for me.

When it comes to being a road dog and developing road-dog relationships, I am undeniably a work in progress. But that's the point of an uncompromising mindset: it doesn't demand perfection, just a commitment to progress.

With that in mind, I've tried to adopt a few aphorisms from Colin Powell that have to do with not letting my failures define my current reality or my future successes.

Powell, the retired four-star general and former secretary of state, used to put pieces of paper under the glass on his desk with his favorite sayings, and he once read a few of them to a journalist. They showed up in an article in *Parade* and became known as Powell's "Thirteen Rules."[33] Here are the first three:

1. "It ain't as bad as you think. It will look better in the morning."
2. "Get mad, then get over it."
3. "It can be done."

Each of those reminds me of another adage: it's never too late to do the right thing. And the right thing is to invest in relationships.

As I've grown to appreciate the importance of meaningful relationship, I've gotten better at living out those aphorisms.

This shift for me was evident, for instance, when Teddy Snowden, one of the members of Unique, Inc., reemerged in my life. None of us had seen or heard from Teddy in years. We didn't know if we'd done something wrong or what. We just knew he disengaged from the group until Ron Singletary, who lives in Dallas, started a "virtual Sunday School" class during the 2020 pandemic. And guess who joined us? Teddy.

Ten years earlier, I might not have been interested in welcoming him back with open arms, or I might have jumped up to ask where he had been all those years. But by this time in my life, I had matured enough to know none of that mattered. All that mattered was that he was my friend and he was back. I was genuinely excited to renew the relationship, and I didn't stress a bit about what

---

33 Colin Powell, *It Worked for Me: In Life and Leadership* (New York: Harper Perennial, 2014).

had kept him away. If he wanted or needed to share, I'd be there. But I felt no desire to press the issue.

I've come to realize that just because I haven't always been good at deep relationships, that doesn't mean I shouldn't work hard at it today. I'm not as bad at it as I think, and I'll be better at it in the morning. If things go wrong, it's OK to get mad as long as I get over it. And if I keep at it, it can be done.

ENRICHING YOU ENRICHES ME

There's a counterintuitive reality about relationships that I had to embrace before I could fully appreciate their power in my life.

As a businessman, I prefer to see numbers that add up. In simple terms, if revenues don't exceed expenses, then we've got a problem. If we don't earn a profit, we can't stay in business. The math needs to make sense for me to move forward. But here's the thing about relationships: they have a math problem.

Think of it this way: If I have a hundred dollars in my money clip and I give you twenty, the math tells me I am twenty dollars poorer and you are twenty dollars richer. But in relationships, whatever I cheerfully and unconditionally give to you somehow multiplies in ways that make us both better off.

This reality about the multiplying value of relationships hit home when a friend told me the story of her involvement with a small university that primarily serves kids from the inner city. She believed in the work this university was doing, so she decided to make financial contributions to support it. But when she told the development director she was sending a check, he didn't just say *thank you* and start filling out a deposit slip. He asked her a question: *Would you like to meet your students?*

That simple invitation led to something powerful: personal interactions that resulted in personal relationships. My friend not only continued to give financially, but she later joined the university's board and eventually became its chair. For her, the work became more meaningful. She was enriching the lives of those students, but her life was being enriched as well—not just because of the results of her work, but even more so because of the relationships she was making.

When she told me that story, I felt a tinge of regret because it made me think of a specific time when I failed to reap the full benefits of investing in relationships.

Shortly after we moved to Denver, I joined the board of the Denver Scholarship Foundation, a nonprofit that helps students in the Denver Public Schools enroll in and graduate from college. It not only provides scholarships, it also provides students with things like mentors, advisors, and tutors who help ensure their success.

I was on that board for seven years, and I saw the organization impact thousands of lives. I'm proud of the contributions I made, but I was mainly involved with the board— not the students. Make no mistake: volunteering with DSF enriched my life, and I got more out of it than I put into it. But I also missed a chance to tap into a bigger multiplying factor by simply making a few more personal deposits into relationships.

That, I've discovered, is really the key to cultivating meaningful relationships: to consistently make deposits into the lives of others. Not just my existing road dogs, but everyone I meet. My time, energy, wisdom, and even my money might appear to be a gift that I'm giving away, but they are really an investment. And when I make those deposits, especially in personal, relational ways, the returns defy mathematical logic. It's like me handing you that twenty in the morning and mysteriously discovering at the end of the day that we're both fifty dollars richer.

What do we get? Well, it depends. We might actually reap some sort of tangible, measurable reward. Investing in relationships often leads someone to donate to a charity we're promoting, give us a good recommendation that lands us a client, or buy us a nice Christmas present. But there's something more, something indescribably priceless that comes from these deposits—we get a *feeling*.

There are no guarantees that people will appreciate the deposits we make in their lives, much less reciprocate in some way that benefits us directly. If that's our expectation, then we're setting ourselves up for disappointment. But if we find joy in the giving, that's more than enough. We can receive whatever else might come as a bonus, but our happiness doesn't depend on someone else's actions.

When I was growing up, for instance, I took part in a mentoring program where I was assigned a "big brother." This young African American executive spent time with me for about a year, taking me to ball games and such. The relationship didn't last long, but it had an enduring impact. He modeled professionalism in the way he dressed and the way he spoke. He showed me what it looked like to be calm, cool, and confident. And he helped me expand the expectations I had for my future.

I doubt that big brother has any idea what became of me, and I have no idea whether he walked away from our time together feeling a sense of joy. But I know this: his deposits made me a better person, so I hope he reaped the rewards of his selflessness.

All of our deposits don't result in road-dog relation-ships, but it's impossible to develop road-dog relationships without making these types of deposits. The good news is that we don't have to end up with a road-dog relationship to reap the benefits of our deposits. If we enrich the lives of others, it will always enrich our lives as well.

DEVELOPING AN INVESTMENT MINDSET

After more than thirty years together, I still don't have permission to take my wife for granted. In fact, there will never come a day when I can stop making deposits in our relationship. As she gently reminds me from time to time: "Date me, dude!"

The same is true of all relationships, but especially those that eventually reach road-dog status. Relationships are not static. They are not a destination we reach. They are ever-evolving. And while some aspects of nurturing a relationship might get easier with time, we can never stop making new deposits.

It's pretty clear that making these deposits pays huge dividends, but we also can agree that it's often hard to make those investments on a consistent basis. For me, there are at least three main reasons for that struggle. Perhaps you can relate.

One, it often involves a perceived personal sacrifice. We have to give up something of value like our time or our money when we invest in someone else. Letting go of things we think we own isn't easy, because we're prone to focus more on what we think we're losing than what we stand to gain.

Two, it often involves uncomfortable levels of transparency. As my friend Walt Rakowich puts it, we have to be authentic and open a window into our souls.[34] When we are that transparent, we tend to fear people will judge us harshly, fairly or unfairly, and we don't want to open ourselves up to potential abuse or ridicule. Or we feel they will betray our trust, so we'd rather not take that risk.

And, three, it often involves what Kim Scott, an author and former executive at both Google and Apple, calls "radical candor."[35] This is the difference between having a lap-dog who adds value mainly by making us feel good and a road dog who will bark in our face and might even bite us in the behind when necessary to get our attention. In other words, we have to speak hard truths to people and accept the hard truths they speak to us, and that's not easy to do.

Because building meaningful relationships is not easy, it demands a fiercely independent, radically responsible, scrappy, and undistracted mindset. In my commitment to this pathway, there are a few concepts that help me push past those challenges so I am more willing to focus on the value rather than the perceived sacrifices, get uncomfortable in my transparency, and embrace hard truths as meaningful deposits.

Walk two dogs at the same time.

There's a misconception that pervades much of life that tells us we must always see things as either/or when they really are both/and. It's like saying you can only walk this dog or that dog when you really can walk both dogs at the same time.

---

34 Walt Rakowich, *Transfluence: How to Lead with Transformative Influence in Today's Climates of Change* (Nashville, TN: Post Hill Press, 2020).
35 Kim Scott, *Radical Candor: Be a Kick-ass Boss Without Losing Your Humanity* (New York: St. Martin's Press, 2019).

Developing an investment mindset about relationships means realizing that concepts like giving hard feedback and loving someone aren't mutually exclusive, either/or propositions. I can give you hard feedback with love. In fact, because I love you, I will always tell you what you need to hear, not just what you want to hear. And if I know you love me, I'm more willing to accept what you tell me, even if it's not what I was hoping to hear.

Real friends, for instance, will tell you the truth about your big-dream idea without crushing your big dream. Rather than saying you are crazy and your idea will never work, they reframe it. They ask relevant questions, and they point out the costs that you might have overlooked. They help you define the steps you'll have to take to succeed. They bathe you in reality so that you can't say, "I didn't know better." They tell you the truth *and* support you in your journey.

There's magic in relationships where we're free to tell each other what we need to hear and not just what we want to hear. Our blind spots disappear, we are able to change our unproductive behaviors, and we can live more meaningful lives.

This mindset requires consistency. If I haven't made deposits that show I care about you as a person, my critiques will come off poorly and won't be well received—even if they are accurate. But if I've consistently walked both dogs at the same time, you are more likely to embrace the feedback.

Again, this type of mindset also helps you receive truth from others. When I was Comcast's regional leader for California, for instance, I developed a strong enough relationship with my team that they weren't afraid to disagree with me.

You might recall that this was my "dress rehearsal" period—I knew the West Division president planned to retire and my performance in California was key to getting a shot as his replacement. During that time, we were considering a plan to centralize our dispatch centers, and I saw this as a potential big win both for me and the company. It held the potential for huge savings for Comcast and an improved customer experience, so I was all gung-ho for going forward with it.

Marty Robinson and Hank Fore, two members of my management team, saw some flaws in the timing, however, and they weren't shy about telling me.

Boss, we'll follow you wherever you take us, they said, *but we're convinced that doing this now is not the right thing.*

They told me why, of course, and that was important in my decision to delay the initiative. But we never would have gotten to the why if they had been afraid to push back against my enthusiasm or if I had responded to their opinions with anger or a dismissive attitude.

Listen...and speak. Give...and receive.

Relationships require a harmony of interactions, and there are times when we sing different parts. We know the importance of listening (two ears, one mouth) and we know the value of giving. Yet in a relationship, there also are times when we need to speak and times when we need to receive what others can give.

For many of us, the "giving" part is easy. We don't have trouble donating to a friend's charity, making a phone call to connect them with someone who can help with their business, or recommending a restaurant. And we're quick to speak truth directly into their lives when we see that it could help and that they are open to it. Maybe they are walking off course and we need to remind them of all the things they've told us are important to them. We can do that, no problem.

We also might be pretty good at listening. We can ask open-ended questions and pause, listening to someone who needs to get their troubles off their chest. When I have one-on-one meetings, I almost always start with a few questions that free the other person to share what's going on in his or her life. I usually ask two or three follow-up questions as well. I'm genuinely interested, and I've become pretty good at asking and listening.

The harder part for me is sharing about my troubles, describing my faults, and receiving the wise counsel and advice of friends. I think many people are like that. Maybe we don't want to appear weak or vulnerable, but we'll never grow to our full potential if we don't open ourselves up to the right advisors (be selective) and share the deeper challenges of our journey.

I've found that time and place are critical components of this part of the pathway. Once you begin developing a relationship with that level of trust, you have to be strategic and intentional about when and where you have conversations that go beyond news, weather, and sports. Maybe it's over coffee one morning or during a weekend getaway where there's time for fun activities but also time to relax and talk.

Too many relationships are defined around the activities—let's play golf, play basketball, go to a football game, or whatever—and they allow no time for discussions about things in life that really matter. Make the time. Find the right place.

Work together to win together.

You no doubt have heard all about the importance of creating win-win scenarios. That's all well and good, but it's not always "best." In a win-win scenario, one side wins and the other side wins, right? But while both sides walk away with a sense of victory, it still means the two sides were competing against each other.

When we make deposits in our relationships, however, we aren't on different sides in a battle—we're on the same team. When I invest in other people or when they are investing in me, I try to see our relationship in the metaphor of a team, not two competitors. We can sit together at the table of prosperity and both fully enjoy the meal. We each might have to make perceived sacrifices along the way, but we'll do that for the team to win. Then we realize there was no real sacrifice, just an investment into the shared victory.

This part of my investment mindset as a leader showed up often during my career, because I had the opportunity to work with hundreds of direct reports over the years.

I did my best to help each of them become a better leader and achieve their personal goals, and I was very intentional in how I went about it. For instance, with my direct reports, I worked to have a personal relationship that wasn't a personal friendship. That meant, for instance, that I learned all I could about their families and their personal dreams, but I maintained objectivity about my role as a supervisor (another example of walking two dogs at the same time).

I also was intentional in making plans that would help them. I allocated consistent time to learn about what mattered to them in their journey. Professionally, I started from the end point—when their career was over, what would they like to have accomplished?—and then we built a plan toward those goals. The plan included things like creating exposure to certain experiences, getting them into the right training programs, and connecting them with the right people and resources.

When you take this approach, of course, you have to be prepared for the reality that people eventually will develop beyond what you can offer. I had to see it as a win, in other words, when my direct reports won opportunities that took them off my team.

Jeff Allen was one of those direct reports who won an opportunity that cost our team his services. Jeff was a key reason we were able to grow Comcast Business, one of our business units, from $229 million to $2.6 billion over an eleven-year period. He started as our business operations leader and ultimately was promoted to senior vice president to lead the entire business unit. He was extremely good at his work.

In 2016, however, Jeff expressed his desire to do something different. We had developed a transparent relationship, so I wasn't surprised that he was longing to start his own company and carve his own path. In fact, we had worked to ensure many of his assignments with Comcast prepared him for taking this leap. Now that he felt ready, we worked together on a one-year transition plan that allowed me to support him while also putting a succession plan in place. And in 2017, he cofounded Nodin, a software as a service company that helps businesses turn data into insights.

Having a work-together-to-win-together mindset about our relationship not only helped Jeff prepare for that role, but it helped Comcast and it helped me. I believe it brought out the best in Jeff while he was with Comcast because he felt valued. I took joy in helping him pursue his dream—helping him reinforced my why of creating a table of prosperity for others. I also think I developed a reputation as a leader that top talent wanted to work for, which helped us plan and execute a smooth transition when Jeff left.

MAKING THE MOST OF RELATIONSHIPS

Tommy Spaulding describes relationships on a spectrum of intimacy and trust. On one end, you have what he calls first-floor (transactional) relationships. You don't really know the other person, but you are interacting briefly in a transactional way like when you pay for coffee at the airport. But the more you get to know and trust another person, the more the relationship moves beyond surface-level topics. And some develop into what he calls fifth-floor (transformational) relationships.[36]

Tommy is the undisputed king of fifth-floor relationships. He earns trust because he is transparent about who he is, genuine in his desire to help others, and trustworthy with the confidences he keeps and the commitments he makes.

What's most unique to me about Tommy, though, is that he can have that type of relationship with dozens and dozens of friends. I'm not Tommy. Never will be, frankly. We have different personalities, different strengths, and different weaknesses. But I am inspired by Tommy to add

---

36 Tommy covers this in detail in his first book, *It's Not Just Who You Know: Transform Your Life (and Your Organization) by Turning Colleagues and Contacts into Lasting, Genuine Relationships* (New York: Crown Business, 1994).

more value to the relationships I'm in, and that's what this pathway is all about.

Yes, I need more road dogs in my life, but it's not just about that. It's about valuing other people and relationships so highly that I instinctively make and receive deposits that add to their lives and mine. When I do that, some relationships will naturally rise to a higher level, and I need to embrace those opportunities and pursue them.

If I am uncompromisingly on this pathway, the dividends at times might be hard to define, but I know one word that accurately describes them—legacy. In fact, when all the seven pathways we've discussed merge together, that's where they lead—to a legacy that's not about us but that leaves an enduring, positive difference on the world.

Chapter 10

What's in Your Box?

BARBITA WAS PREGNANT IN 2012 when I discovered what I guess has become a new cultural norm: you don't have to be a woman to get a baby shower.

The fact that we were having a child was big news in our work and social circles, because, as I've previously mentioned, we had been trying for years to add to our family. Once the pregnancy moved into the second trimester, we felt it was safe to share the joyful news that we were expecting a baby boy and that we planned to name him Steven Andrew White II.

Barbita's friends had a baby shower for her in October, and I figured that was the end of that. I had always thought these parties were just for women and that the biggest benefit they provided to men was an afternoon or evening to watch sports or action movies. But, lo and behold, my senior leadership team at Comcast threw a baby shower, and I was the guest of honor.

It was December, about a week before Stevie was born, and I was leading a monthly planning session in our Denver office. When it was time for lunch, we headed to a conference room to eat, and I was surprised to find balloons and cake to go with the food. Frankly, it was a little awkward, because about half of my team was men, but it was also fun. We ate and we socialized, and then I took the seat of honor for the more formal part of the party.

First, they had a little fun at my expense. The group had collaborated on a "top ten list" of things our unborn son needed to know to prepare for life with me as his dad, so they began by reading that letter. Let's just say there wasn't much advice in it that I wanted Stevie to follow!

Number 1 was "It's OK to cry when you see him—the one thing in life you can't pick is your father." They made fun of my penchant for neatness, especially when it comes to my car, by advising Stevie to "get comfortable and make sure you have lots of drinks and snacks when you travel." They knew I was apprehensive about changing diapers, so they suggested Stevie try a diet of Gerber's "Fig and Shrimp." They also knew I'm not a dog guy, so they told him no childhood is complete without a puppy (and they added a photo of a Saint Bernard).

You get the idea.

When the roasting was over, I opened the gifts and showed them off to everyone in the room. I appreciated them all, of course, but one stood out among the others, and it came from the entire group: a box.

It was a really nice box, too. I don't know how much it cost, but I can tell you it was not cheap. It's made of silver, the lid latches and locks, and the initials "SAW" are engraved on the top. It looks incredibly classy sitting on a shelf near my desk in my home office.

The real value of the box, however, has nothing to do with the quality of the container and everything to do with its contents. The things inside that box cost my coworkers nothing, and, yet, they are priceless.

I'll never forget opening that gift. I took it out and looked it over, examining the top, bottom, and each side, thinking to myself, *What the heck is this?* Then I carefully unhinged the latch, lifted the lid, and peeked in to see what was there.

Cards?

Pulling out the first card, I realized the box had a dozen or so handwritten notes from the people on my team. They were addressed to "Steven A. White."

Not me, but Stevie.

Unlike the playful top-ten list they had read earlier, these were heartfelt notes that shared with him some of the things they appreciated about his father. And in doing that, they gave me one of the most precious gifts I've ever received—a tangible affirmation that working through a lifetime of exhaustion was worth all the effort and that my uncompromising philosophy had helped me achieve my why—not just in my mind, but in the minds of others who knew me.

I read them all, each one slowly and emotionally, realizing that they were both a compliment to the life I had lived to that point and a challenge to be the man these coworkers were describing.

I've read those notes several times over the years, and I reflected on what they said as I worked on the outline for this book. The notes in many ways illustrate the importance of my seven pathways—find your fight, focus on the (real) prize, live life as a learning lab, think and act like a business, own your attitude and effort, navigate uncertainty, and commit to road-dog relationships.

For instance, when one person wrote, "Your father is a teacher...and he will teach you the right values and how to succeed in life," it reminded me of my commitment to live life as a learning lab.

Another wrote, "He earned his way, and no doubt he will require you to earn yours. He will use this to teach you that nothing is achieved without some degree of sacrifice and pain. The good news is that he will help you develop the disciplines you need to withstand it all." I think that speaks to focusing on the real prize and owning your attitude and effort.

Yet another wrote, "Even if he doesn't love your first idea, keep trying. He'll listen, and he can change his mind," and then added, "He gave me a shot, inspiring me to be on top of my game every day, and I know he'll inspire you to do the same." Those ideas relate to learning, navigating uncertainty, and being a road dog.

More than one message made me think of what it means to create a table of prosperity for others.

One wrote, "He is a man who is driven to make a difference in people's lives through his vision, passion, and ability to make things happen through others." And another, addressing it to me but for Stevie to read, wrote, "Through all of the ups and downs of the business over the course of the years, one thing has remained consistent: Your dedication to and focus on my personal development, growth, and career has always been a priority of yours. I thank you. Little Stevie will be very fortunate to have that in his dad."

I know in my heart how often I have fallen short of those types of praises. I haven't always lived with a fiercely independent, radically responsible, scrappy, and undistracted mindset. I haven't always had an unwavering commitment to my why. So there have been plenty of missed opportunities, plenty of times when I failed to live in an uncompromising fashion. But I felt honored that they saw examples of the man I've aspired to be in the actions of the person they had worked with each day. And it was affirming to know my approach had produced at least a few things that they felt were worth passing along to Stevie.

The challenge, of course, is to live up to them myself.

You might recall way back in the opening pages of this book that I mentioned how the pressure to live up to that type of challenge has contributed to my lifetime of exhaustion as a black male striving to succeed in the corporate world. But here's the good news: learning to embrace an uncompromising approach to life hasn't contributed to that exhaustion. Instead, it's worked against it. It's helped me find rest and peace, because an uncompromising mindset has helped me grow confident in my why and in the belief that giving my best to those pathways is enough.

I can never fully live up to the expectations I've felt over my lifetime, expectations from myself as well as from others, but I can commit to win at life each day the right way.

I've discovered over the decades that there are plenty of wrong ways to win in life. You don't have to look far to see examples of men and women who have lied, cheated, and stolen their way to the top. They have used and abused people to fatten their bank accounts. They have cut corners and fudged a few numbers on the spreadsheets so that they can live in big homes, drive expensive cars, wear fancy clothes, and go on fabulous vacations. They have given to others, but only if it somehow benefited their selfish purposes, like to make them look good in the eyes of the public.

That's not the way I want to win in life. I want to win the right ways. And in my experience, the right ways are grounded in an uncompromising commitment to those pathways—a commitment to doing my best and refocusing and recommitting whenever I get sidetracked. That is what leads to something special. That is what leads to an impactful life and meaningful legacy.

When I die, my body will likely end up in an overpriced box in a mausoleum. But I hope the legacy of my uncompromising life is represented in the letters found in the small silver box that I'll one day pass along to my son—what one group of people at one moment in time believed to be true about me, my impact on their lives, and the type of father they expected I would be.

When I'm gone, everyone I've touched with my life will have an opinion about whether my influence was positive or negative. If I found my fight, stayed focused on what matters, always tried to learn new things, invested in myself like a business, owned my attitude and effort, navigated uncertainty, and committed to road-dog relationships—if I had some measure of consistency on those pathways—then people around me will have benefited and my life will have mattered to others.

More importantly, I will have lived a life that honored the gift of grace I was given in 1997 when I rededicated my life to God. That's when my fight was supercharged by a relationship and my reason for serving others became tied to the love that I have been given rather than love I was trying to earn. Instead of fighting to prove my worth, I was fighting to show my gratitude.

For me, the whole point of an uncompromising approach to the twisting journey of life is so we can joyfully make a difference in the lives of the people around us—our family, our friends, our employees and coworkers, and our community at large. If we do that consistently, our box will be filled with a legacy that matters.

So, I ask you: What's in your box?

My goal with this book has been to help you learn from my experiences, the good as well as the myriad challenges that, when added up, created the exhaustion I've described in my journey. Your challenges might look similar or totally different. But like my exhaustion, they hold the potential of hampering how well you will fight for your why and whether you will live an uncompromising life. If you can replicate the things that will make your life more meaningful and impactful and avoid (when possible) some of the ditches, then I'm convinced you will overcome your challenges and like what's in your box.

I've shared what I've learned on my journey, because I want to create a table of prosperity where everyone can participate and enjoy life. But that means you can't just read this book and set it aside. You need to take what you've learned, apply it, improve upon it, and, most importantly, share those lessons with others and guide them on their journeys.

Find your fight, and then help them find their fight and live it with a fiercely independent, radically responsible, scrappy, and undistracted mindset. Whatever you do, don't compromise on that challenge. Start living it today. Create your own tables of prosperity.